SPIRITUAL
INITIATION
AND THE
BREAKTHROUGH
OF
CONSCIOUSNESS

Other Books by Joseph Chilton Pearce
published by Park Street Press

The Biology of Transcendence
The Crack in the Cosmic Egg
From Magical Child to Magical Teen

SPIRITUAL INITIATION

AND THE

BREAKTHROUGH

OF

CONSCIOUSNESS

THE BOND OF POWER

JOSEPH CHILTON PEARCE

Park Street Press

Rochester, Vermont

Park Street Press
One Park Street
Rochester, Vermont 05767
www.InnerTraditions.com

Park Street Press is a division of Inner Traditions International

Originally published in 1981 by Elsevier-Dutton Publishing Co., Inc. under the title
The Bond of Power. Published simultaneously in 1981 in Canada by Clarke,
Irwin & Company Limited, Toronto and Vancouver.

LIBRARY OF CONGRESS CATALOGING-IN-PUBLICATION DATA
Pearce, Joseph Chilton.
Spiritual initiation and the breakthrough of
consciousness : the bond of power / Joseph Chilton Pearce.
p. cm.
Includes bibliographical references.
ISBN 0-89281-995-2
1. Spirituality—Psychology. I. Title.
BL624.P425 2003
291.4'2—dc21
2003012395

Printed and bound in the United States at Lake Book Manufacturing, Inc.

10 9 8 7 6 5 4 3 2 1

Text design by Nicola Mazzella

To
Shelley Scott Mullenix
whose persistent letters
led the way

The force that through the green fuse drives the flower
Drives my green age; that blasts the roots of trees
Is my destroyer.
And I am dumb to tell the crooked rose
My youth is bent by the same wintry fever . . .

from
"The Force That Through the Green
Fuse Drives the Flower"
DYLAN THOMAS

Taking the form of a bird,
He sings in the trees . . .
Through Him, the buried seed sprouts into a plant.
Through Him, the hair grows on your head . . .
Whatever you do, it is only through Him . . .
He is the source of all your actions . . .

from
Reflections of the Self
MUKTANANDA

Contents

SPIRITUAL
INITIATION
AND THE
BREAKTHROUGH
OF
CONSCIOUSNESS

Introduction

In some off-guard moment, a thought which illuminates new territory can explode in our heads and change the shape of our thinking and our lives. This "postulate which arrives full-blown in the brain" is a function of mind which holds the key to our nature, development, and fulfillment.

This phenomenon is rare. It comes as creative inspiration, scientific discovery, the Eureka!, the mystical revelation, the conversion experience. Its source has been a matter of debate. Trace the function *to* its source, though, and the mystery of our brain, mind, creation, and creator unfolds. The postulate is like a thread which, pulled from the woof and warp of our reality, unweaves that fabric and leaves us the threads from which reality itself is woven.

The problem with tracing the roots of creative insight is that thought, no matter its strength or brilliance, is not sufficient for the task. The postulate-revelation doesn't arrive in the brain *as* thought, but as the materials *for* thought. Thought is but a tool of the function and seems only peripherally (though vitally) involved.

Revelation is as valid a term as postulate, since new information seems revealed to our mind, rather than thought by it. The postulate seems to arise from some deep recess of mind, not brain. I will use the term *insight* hereafter, since it is a "seeing" from within, even when projected without.

For instance, Kekulé, the famous chemist, "saw" a ring of snakes with their tails in their mouths, directly in front of him, for a historic instant. Translated into the language of his profession, that configuration gave us the benzene ring, basis of all modern chemistry (for good or ill).

Insight seems extracerebral, an intrusion into our awareness. It flashes into us always in some moment out of mind, never when we are busy thinking about the subject involved. The great mathematician, William Hamilton, received his insight into the Quaternion Theory while crossing the bridge into Dublin one morning. The solution arrived in that instant when thought of quaternions was the furthest thing from his mind.

Insight seems enormously powerful when it arrives. At times it breaks right through our thinking and ordinary perceptions. This power gives insight its numinous, mystical edge of awesomeness and conviction to its recipients. This power emboldens us to act on the revelation in spite of its novelty or improbable nature, and gives us the strength to carry it into the common domain against odds.

Insight seems a *grace,* that which is given freely rather than made by our effort. Einstein spoke of his insights arriving like flashes of lightning which, though they lit up the landscape of his mind for only an instant, forever after changed its shape. The only thing which can change the nature of our thought is an energy more powerful than that thought. So there are different modes of mental experience and the difference lies in the levels of energy involved.

Ordinary thinking, our everyday "roof-brain chatter," is a weak-energy emergent of our brain, while insight is surely more powerful. That is why the insight function isn't reversible, to be repeated by formula. Our ordinary thinking can (must) prepare for insight, respond to it, but can't manufacture it. A weak thought can't produce a stronger one, but it can attract it.

Nothing that we can do will insure the arrival of insight, yet insight comes to us only when we are passionately involved in the subject matter concerned, and have thoroughly prepared for its coming. Kekulé, for instance, had passionately sought for the secret of the benzene ring. Hamilton had spent fifteen years searching for the mathematical key to the quaternions before his bridge-revelation. Einstein, as a young man, had set out with a passion to find some unity of time, space, and matter.

William Blake said "Mechanical excellence is the vehicle for genius." Genius is our personal realm of insight. Insight is the grace given, the stuff of genius, but a grace had at the price of passion, unbending intent, will, hard work, and tenacity.

In his mature years, Mozart's mechanical excellence was so perfected that his genius could speak as direct insight. He would receive a commission for a new symphony and the work was quite likely to fall into his head as a gestalt, arrive full-blown in his brain, twenty minutes of music in an instant out of time. He then had the arduous task of translating that moment out of mind into the myriad of notes which could, in turn, be translated by others to make the symphony sound in the actual world.

A pianist friend of mine was preparing to play his favorite Mozart sonata in concert one evening. He leaned back to immerse himself in the nature of that work, and experienced the entire sonata as a single "round volume of sound." Every note, phrase, and nuance was there, perfect and complete in that instant out of time. The experience was numinous, of a religious, mystical tinge, and had a profound effect on my friend. He had, perhaps, shared the sonata's original nature as insight-revelation.

The task of translating insight often proves as great as the work necessary to bring it about. Hamilton spent fifteen years on the quaternions *after* his insight. Kekulé's translation bridging the symbolism of a ring of snakes to the hard data of chemistry was not simple, nor was Einstein's final neat equation spelled out in that original lightning bolt.

Back in 1958, I had a minor insight which followed, in my own minor way, the classical pattern of all insight. My insight was, in effect, a glimpse into the mechanics of insight itself. Being of a slow mind (and with four children to raise), it took me some twelve years to finish a translation. The end-result was my book *The Crack in the Cosmic Egg*. In that book I outlined a fourfold procedure found in any creative venture, discovery, or transformation experience resulting in insight. Since that "formula of creativity" is a way to trace insight to its roots, I will summarize it here:

First, to entice insight into our lives, we must be caught up in some passionate quest. (No dilettantes here.) A certain intensity of purpose must be generated which finally swamps our switchboard, absorbs all our attention, rules out our lesser goals and passions. Then we must work for that mechanical excellence which alone can serve as the vehicle of our genius. We must gather the materials related to, and develop the abilities needed by, our quest. If an artist, we must perfect the mechanics of our art; as a scientist we must thoroughly search the area of our interest; as philosophers we must gather all possible pertinent knowledge; as spiritual seekers we must immerse ourselves completely in our chosen path. The half-hearted endeavor will leave us with only our weak thought and vain imaginings.

Our passionate pursuit, which may take months or years, must feed a massive amount of material into the hopper of our mind/brain. The materials must then at some point "take over," take on a life of their own, dictate their own ends, overrule even the person gathering them. We must feel subservient to our own pursuit, used by it, incidental to it. This ushers in the "gestation period," when the mass of accumulated data and/or ability achieves its critical size and power. Then, within that mysterious realm of insight, the revelation will form. Maybe.

In order to unfold as revelation in the brain, insight must get thought out of the way, at least for the brief instant needed. So the insight arrives in some moment of suspended thought, or simply pushes thought briefly aside.

Only an instant is needed for insight to break through since it comes always as a single unit, not in some digital breakdown. Insight is always complete and perfect in its single instant's appearance, for it is a wholeness, or a power, that can't be divided. It appears in all-or-nothing form.

The final stage is our translation of that insight into the common domain. This task may be frustrating, for verbal thinking is a weak tool for handling such power. Our translation is often clumsy and may seem a poor substitute for the pristine purity of our original vision. The numinous power of the revelation generally sustains us in our attempts, however, and the final expression in a language is the measure of our genius. The greater our mechanical excellence, the stronger our intelligence, the greater the possibilities our genius can express through us.

In recent years, research has indicated a division of labor in our mind/brain, between spatial wholes and digital breakdowns. This is the well-worn theory of right and left brain-thinking. Our preoccupation, indeed isolation within, left-hemisphere, or digital, analytical "take-apart" thinking, has been the subject of much speculation. While insight clearly indicates a mode of unity-thinking, in contrast to analytical thinking, a look at the whole procedure shows interaction between the two disparate modes. Insight indicates a greater power than thinking, involves a wider spectrum of mind/brain activity, but synchrony of the two also takes place.

Imbalance of right and left thinking seems to bring about dysfunctions. In my book *Magical Child,* I discussed some of the critical problems facing technological countries today. These conditions are apparently brought about by imbalances of thought connected with technology itself. The problems I addressed in my book have worsened sharply in the four years since I completed it, until any hope of solution seems remote to our time. (I need only mention the continuing epidemic increase of infantile autism; childhood schizophrenia; brain damage and its mental-physical dysfunctions in general; infant-child abuse; the collapse of the family unit; the increase of suicides in children; the breakdown in classroom discipline and inability of young people to learn; these coupled with a general increase in social collapse and adult confusion.)

Technology is sweeping our earth, and our social-mental breakdown seems an outgrowth of that sweep, indicating a mode of thinking out of balance and out of control. As usual in imbalance, our attempts at redress lead only to extremes equally unbalanced. Technology seems here to stay and the issue isn't how to get rid of it (which we don't want to do even though we sometimes hate it) but how to achieve balance with it.

We refer to left-hemisphere thinking, from which science and technology seem to spring, as "dominant thinking." We tacitly assume that such thinking is superior; cultures using less stringent modes of logic crumble before this apparently more powerful intelligence.

Intelligence, however, is the ability to interact, and the ability to interact has not increased through technology. It has decreased. We have long spoken of our technological devices as "extensions" of our personal power: telescopes, microscopes, and so on, extend our vision; telephones and radios our hearing; machines our muscular power; computers our mental ability; weaponry our survival capacity; chemistry our dominion over insects, disease, perhaps even death someday; and so on.

In practice, though, every technological achievement really undermines, erodes, even replaces, in one way or another, our ability it "extends and enhances." Instead of extending and increasing personal power, our devices sharply reduce it. Any reduction of personal power produces anxiety, as millions of years of genetic encoding and expectancies begin to be shortchanged. Thus the paradox that our anxiety has increased proportionately (in fact, widely out of proportion) with our technological "advances" which should, by all rights, *reduce* anxiety.

For instance, even as we have developed the telescope, microscope, television, and so on, personal vision has collapsed correspondingly. There are peoples whose vision is so keen they can see the rings of Saturn with their naked eyes. Contrast this natural endowment with the records of the "visual health" of school children in Texas:

In 1900, when children did not enter school until age eight, one child in every eight had a visual problem (commonly myopia). In 1907, the age was lowered to seven, and ten years later one child in three was myopic. In 1930, the age of attendance was lowered to six, and myopia by 1940 afflicted 50 percent of all children. In the 1950's, television entered the scene, and by 1962, five out of every six children were myopic—almost a complete reversal of the original figures in sixty years.

Surely no one-for-one correspondence can be established between such statistics and any specific cause; the whole social fabric is involved. Yet the correspondence is perfectly valid for the case in point, and the same case can be made for every aspect of human development and our resulting personal power. For a half-century I have heard the daily reports of thrilling new breakthrough discoveries promising perfect health, wealth, and all but eternal life for all, and have watched the quality of life, and psychological-physical health, deteriorate until we are a society in serious trouble.

Learning research finds that anxiety is the great enemy of intelligence and development. So its increase can be seen as an automatic index of a decrease in intelligence. A major thrust today in the medical-drug industry is for so-called "mind-control" drugs, most of which deal with curbing anxiety and depression. Meanwhile, sociologists still note a striking absence of anxiety and depression in the few preliterate or nontechnological societies left on Earth (and we assume they are disappearing from history from their inability to compete intellectually).

Our personal power seems to be draining right out of us into our machinery and tools. Human survival, development, our autonomy as persons, our long-range genetic goals, all center on development of ability, which means personal power. Ages of genetic expectancy are built into us, cued to expect development of personal power. When this vast expectancy begins to sharply erode, anxiety is the only possible result.

Our anxiety is not some passing emotional disturbance, but a biological imbalance flashing its danger-to-survival signals. The result of our anxiety, however, is an increased demand for and production of technological "advances" to "extend our powers" and so relieve that anxiety. This creates a neat, double-bind vicious circle since the end-result is always greater loss of personal power, more anxiety, more demand for further gimmickry, and so on. (Technological childbirth is a prime example. Or, observe, since the advent of air-conditioning, hundreds dying during each heat wave, when their air conditioners fail.)

The threat of technology is no more from bombs or pollution as this growing loss of personal power and our ensuing collapse into anxiety. Anxiety is singularly intolerable to the brain system, truly swamps the switchboard and stops all processes, as everything in an anxiety-ridden brain bends toward trying to *remove* that anxiety.

Anxiety is not some intruder in the mind, though, not some foolish notion or wrong idea. It is a state of mind which acts as a form influencing all sensory and mental content. Anxiety arises from a more powerful modality than ordinary discursive, logical thinking, and its greater energy dwarfs and warps our supposed objectivity. Anxiety aligns our brains into a focus on and service of that anxiety state.

The dominance of left-hemisphere thinking may result then, not from its inherent superiority, but from the anxiety and powerlessness this one-sided mental action produces. This substratum of anxiety in technological man may be the force, or one of the forces, that dominates a less powerful logical system or culture.

Anxiety is peculiarly contagious. It operates below the limen of awareness—it isn't made of thought, but shapes or influences thought. It creates on contact an uneasiness, a dis-ease, a vague wrongness, even guilt. This contagion affects a child immediately, and in the same way infects even a people largely free of anxiety historically. Anxiety is like the Midas touch. Everything the anxiety-ridden mind touches, in its ceaseless push for release from that anxiety, turns into that from which release is sought. All Captain Cook needed to do was touch on some preliterate people and the seeds of that culture's destruction were sown.

Teilhard de Chardin spoke of the Earth as a thinking sphere. Perhaps left-hemisphere thinking characterizes the West, as has been suggested, while some aspects of right-hemisphere thinking are found in some Eastern and preliterate societies. Is it too fanciful to speak of the Western world, with its take-apart thinking, as the equivalent of the left hemisphere of this thinking sphere of Earth?

Needless to say, both modes of thinking are valid and needed, yet either is troubled if dominant. Right-hemisphere thinking can lead to stasis, avoidance of concrete thinking, a retreat from the realities of the physical world. Left-hemisphere thinking can lead to splitting-apart to the point of fragmentation and chaos. A balance between the modes is obviously desirable, the subject of many recent books, and a rather remote possibility.

Carl Jung, on his return from a visit to India in 1937, observed that the Hindu didn't seem to think his thoughts as we do in the

West, but "perceives his thought" as though thought were ready-made outside the brain and simply viewed like any sensory act. Indeed, Jung's notion agrees with Hindu and yogic theory that thoughts are not originated in the brain, but are perceived from a stream of impressions impinging on the brain.

At issue here is not the merit of Western and Eastern logics, but a larger definition of mental experience. The relation of mind, brain, and world is not a one-way street. Traffic moves on many levels and incorporates a surprisingly wide terrain. Insight is surely a perfect example of a level of thought not generated by our ordinary brain process. So the suggestion of a perceptual background which includes thought as one of its components is strange to us and academically suspect, but is demonstrated in insight and can be experienced through meditation.

Brain research indicates that new processes of thought and experience open for us through synchronization of right and left hemispheres of the brain. The attempts of Eastern thought to break into Western logic on some serious level today may indicate the attempt of this thinking sphere of Earth to balance the fragmentations of technology. Because of the way genetic development unfolds, and the way enculturation helps mold our whole brain process, a culture can't lift itself out of its own mind-set no matter how destructive that set becomes. Cultural interaction, however, can bail a culture out, much as one person can sometimes help another. So, as our technology absorbs the world, we may in turn be affected positively by that which we absorb.

Surely cultural interaction is often ridiculous on the surface. Technology is exported not by the serious, high and lofty sentiments of a noble science, but the hurly-burly of quick-rich hustlers willing to sell their grandmothers for a nickel. In turn, Eastern thought is represented all too often by atrocious, bizarre opportunists, drop-outs, and ego-maniacs. Yet the West has its true scientific genius, such as the physicist, David Bohm, and the East has its true genius such as the Siddha meditation teacher, Muktananda.

Amid the nonsense of a world of folly, the great syntheses are made by genius, syntheses which sooner or later, with luck, filter down to the level of the common domain. The following pages attempt to outline the mechanics of our disappearing personal power, as modeled within the most complete theory of reality the West has produced, David Bohm's *holonomic movement,* and in the most complete person I have known, that exemplar of personal and bonding power, Muktananda. The issues they present are threefold: insight, ordinary thinking, and the bonding power that underlies these rather polar modes.

There definitely exists in this world a bonding power that can arc the gap and bring us to wholeness. This bonding power, like insight, is directly within each of us, a part of our mind/brain/world function, inherent in our very genetic development, and the subject of this book. Our age of professionalism prefers that we take some small fragment of a notion or observation, and exhaustively research and present the absolute-final-last-word on it. This is not practical here. Our bonding power doesn't lend itself to so precise a definition. My intent is to point toward a radical shift of orientation available through meditation; the nature of our personal power possible through meditation, and its possible remedial use by our culture. My intent is limited, but the scope encompassed is extravagant. If I suggest certain lines of thought but leave them hanging, so be it. I can only invite the reader to carry through.

No synthesis of East-West thought is even suggested here. Such is beyond my area of competence. (Furthermore, two Sanskrit words in succession put me to sleep.) Nor do I attempt some kind and sympathetic overview of meditation systems and teachers. The results of my four-year plunge into meditation have been so far-reaching for me I haven't the slightest interest in exploring other systems. Why go window-shopping when you have already made an improbably successful purchase? Nor is my attempt here some eclectic, dilettante's survey to show that all meditation roads lead to some grand meditation-Rome. I don't believe they do.

From the standpoint of Western logic, serious logical problems appear in the theory of Siddha meditation. I leave such problems out here not because I have lost my logical discrimination but because my task is to point toward the function, the bond of power involved. (Sufficient task, that.) Siddha meditation is a way of unlocking our lost personal power and establishing our bond with the matrix of our life. It works in spite of logical problems, and work-ability is what counts. Like the bumblebee who, according to the laws of aerodynamics, can't fly, flies remarkably well, Siddha medi-tation works in spite of—and even within—our Western logic, or logical box.

Mixed in with our logic is a phenomenon of mind called "psycho-logical distance." This is a kind of safety factor that lets us double-think. For instance, I had an aunt who loved anything antique or "primitive." Even as she eschewed all vulgar, modern trash, she clasped to her bosom the awfullest old pieces of whittled-out junk if she thought them sufficiently *old.* No matter that it was without taste, form, art, or beauty; psychological distance and a few worm holes gave any object all the aesthetics it needed for her.

The same psychic-distance allows us to attribute greatness, even sainthood or divinity, to someone sufficiently long-dead. But a per-sonal investment, indeed *risk,* seems involved in admitting great-ness, saintliness, or divinity, to someone in the flesh. This is acutely so if that person is accessible, and when we know that person will immediately challenge us to change, to fundamentally transform our life.

Psychic-distance allows us to entertain talk of change. How we love to dabble in human potentials, spiritual searches, personal growth-development proposals, consciousness-expansion devices, sensory-enhancement courses, mind-controls, and so on, boosting the morale of, but leaving untouched, our anxiety ridden social-ego. Part of the enormous fascination Carlos Castaneda's Don Juan held for us was in Don Juan's very *un*availability. Reading of him both fed our hope-syndrome, yet kept at bay the awful effort of his transformation. (I don't think this was Castaneda's intent at all, and am convinced we received a great gift from him.[1]) In the pages that follow, this margin of safety doesn't exist and I must risk a credibil-ity gap from the outset.

For the sake of brevity few details are given of the persons in-volved here. I have used David Bohm's magnificent theory (in my own way) but have left Bohm as a person alone. Bohm was a pro-tégé of Einstein's; his book on quantum mechanics is standard text the world over; he is probably one of our century's great creative thinkers and has been a personal hero of mine since his publication, in 1957, of *Causality and Chance in Modern Physics,* surely a milestone of Western thought. For the past decade or so he has been closely associated with Krishnamurti, that most Western of Eastern thinkers.

My own life has undergone serious shifts of orientation as a result of my personal experience with Siddha meditation and its teacher, Muktananda. My shift of orientation marks the point of departure for all that follows in this book, yet I have devoted all of three very brief paragraphs to Muktananda. (If the reader wants more information on Bohm, Muktananda, or Siddha meditation, a brief bibliography is included.)

A bit of public exposure seems called for to get into the materials involved here. I have condensed these personal events to a minimum, not to be coy or hint at Castaneda-type esoterica, but for the sake of brevity. The power of the bond is the issue and my personal experiences are mere springboards to get to the matter at hand. The episodes of the first chapter help to fill the gap between my last book, *Magical Child,* and this one, and may help to show how the bond of power within us will use any and every means available to get through our stupidities and arrogance.

Aside from the opening, this book isn't autobiographical because the issue isn't so much what happened to me as something that may be trying to happen in the world. We have long envisioned a certain balance of mind, a synchrony of brain hemispheres, and, as within—so without. This may be a global vision as well. But balance is achieved not by our efforts to counter one mode of thought by another. It is achieved through a balancing power, a function of wholeness that is a third force in the apparent dual nature of our mind/brain and our world. This third force is a bonding power which holds everything together, from atoms to brains, a kind of universal *corpus callosum.* This force is of incredible, incalculable dimensions, but we are both functional parts of it, partakers in and of it, and in a very vital sense, "spokesmen" for that whole.

This function broke through the rigidity of my brain and my own brand of psychic-distance buffering. It came through a person because real change can take place only through persons (not histories of theories). And I could grasp it as personal power because it came through a person *of* power.

The remedial process that must follow may have a long way to go within me (sigh!) but my freedom from anxiety has already been dramatic and beneficial beyond statement. My wish, then, is that what happened for me, bringing about this book, might happen for some of those chancing to read this little work. Then this skirmish between my typewriter and myself will not have been in vain.

I

Playful Insight

Once a culture or a person collapses into anxiety, no self-effort is effective against that negative power. Only insight has the power to override that negativity and bring the system into balance. Operation bootstrap always fails. Wholeness of mind can't come from any action or thought from a split person, but only through a kind of grace, the power of insight arriving full-blown in the brain.

Whether Kekulé's ring of snakes, Einstein's lightning, or what have you, the function of insight works according to its pattern. Put a sufficient amount of passionate pursuit and collection of materials in, give over personal dominion to those materials, stand back before the insight when it comes, and serve it in its translation you then are empowered to make.

The nature of what we receive is determined by the nature of our output. The genesis of this present book of mine lies in a revelatory experience which came as the culmination to decades of passionate inquiry, even though, as with all insight experience, I surely sowed a wind and reaped a whirlwind. Central to my inquiry was spiritual longing which included religious rejection and rebellion against the idea of God. The focus of these decades finally centered around my work in child development, resulting in my book *Magical Child*, which I completed in 1976. Tangled into this work were strong personal anxiety and a feeling of failure; disturbed recollections on bringing up my four children; the disaster of our fifth child, a cerebral-palsy basket case; emotional residues of the children's mother; her passionate investment in them and early death.

So the book was emotionally charged from the beginning, and I began to give seminars on the subject to get professional feedback and maintain some balance of perspective, since the child theory growing out of the work grew more radical all the time. The seminars were emotionally charged, too, and grew in scope and length until I had to have professional assistance. I hired a full-time director, that I might have time to work on the manuscript while flying about the country giving the seminars.

The central issue of the book and the seminars hinged on child play. I knew developmentalists were wrong to consider child play an attempt to evade the "harsh adjustment to reality." I knew the child didn't play to escape anxiety, but eventually could not play because of anxiety. I knew Piaget was right in his imitation-model theory of play but I knew that, too, was incomplete. The problem was, I didn't know what play *was* all about. I struggled with the issue for months, read all the research available, and became seriously preoccupied with the problem, which seemed a pivot around which all my years of search gravitated.

In the midst of this activity I received a letter from a reader of my previous books. She insisted that I go immediately and meet an Indian "swami," Baba Muktananda. She sent me a picture of the man, as though I couldn't wait.

I receive a certain amount of crank mail; sometimes about various saviors knocking at our doorsteps; sometimes from the self-declared saviors themselves; and more often than not accompanied by pictures, that I might gaze upon their person. But this Muktananda's picture leered up at me like some reckless rock singer, with the most insolent eyes I had ever seen. Most of the would-be holy men at least try to look pious and saintly; this character seemed smug, irreverent, and mocking. I felt a distinct flush of irritation, doubled the mess up and threw it in the wastebasket, without answer.

I had been on a couple of panels with so-called swamis, had met a couple of others accidentally (they seemed everywhere), and had found them a fatuous bunch of egotists. Their copious writings seemed boring, vacuous, irrelevant. A friend and I had laughed smugly over the Guru-of-the-Month Club sweeping the country in the early seventies. I had a serious aversion to the "Indian-trippers" and was pleased with my Western handle on things.

Recently, my former seminar director wrote that back in 1975 she had been going to this very swami, Muktananda, for some six months before taking on the job of my seminars. She had tried, she reports, to tell me something about this man and the remarkable experiences she had undergone as a result of "Shaktipat," or initiation into his meditation practice.[1] My reaction, she wrote, had been so volatile, hostile, indeed irrational (I remember none of this), that she dropped the subject and did not mention it again. (Why cast pearls before swine?)

Thus, even before receiving his picture in the mail, I had been working with a person influenced by and practicing the meditation of this particular Indian teacher. Though I must leap ahead of my argument somewhat here, let me point out that, just as anxiety is peculiarly contagious, because of its negative power, meditation that follows initiation into a powerful system is equally contagious in a positive way. This positive influence had been at work around me, and receipt of the picture worked as a catalyst. In the weeks following my receipt of it, while I worked on my book, read research, or did daily tasks, those insolent eyes would occasionally flash to mind, kicking up the same flush of irritation over tricksters rushing over here to bilk the misguided.

A few weeks later, I sat alone at home one evening, reading a new research paper on play. Suddenly the solution seemed to loom up, right under my nose if my brain would just pull together and clarify matters. But I hadn't the strength of mind. Hours later, drained and defeated by play again, I leaned back, head in hands, and groaned aloud, "Oh God, what *is* the role of play in our life?"

Nothing in my fifty-year history had prepared me for what then happened. Instantly, without warning or transitional change of awareness, shock waves of ecstasy rushed up through my body. Without disturbing my sense of unity, I became aware of each cell in my body as my individual self. There were billions of me in a wild, exuberant dance of joy. Then I felt myself lifted up and hurled, physically it seemed, like a ping-pong ball, from one end of the universe to the other. My body of billions-of-me passed through galaxies of stars, each star also me, pulsing in rhapsodic interaction. Ecstatic wave succeeded wave, each a crescendo of exuberance surpassing the other, and I shouted over and over: "God is playing with me!"

The experience faded without transition of my ordinary consciousness other than to leave me stunned and overwhelmed. I knew then what the role of play was, though, not just in child development, but in all of our life. I was weeks articulating that knowing into words, and rewrote my book on children from that new point. The three-day seminars I was giving on the subject underwent a corresponding change. I became like a smoothly oiled piece of machinery, indefatigable, calm, and certain. I was apparently convincing to others, too, since my seminars grew in demand. My seminar director, whose job was organizing and running the affairs, soon had bookings well in advance.

Amid all this, my interior world was calm but waiting, in a state of suspension. The revelatory experience of play had gone beyond my ordinary understanding and remained an enigma. My previous experiences had been as a candle in the sun compared to this one, even though it, too, followed the classical pattern of Eureka! or conversion. Surely the event had covered the subject of play, but it had also gone vastly beyond. The impact of the experience was too personal and dramatic to dismiss as simply a postulate-response to the materials of my book; too urgent to my immediate life to dismiss as illusion or "subjective delusion," as our petty psychologies might say (in evading the issue); and surely the event had been too joyful to simply abandon and forget.

Further, I knew that even the greatest magician can't pull a rabbit out of the hat unless there is first a rabbit in that hat. As Blake said: "A cup can't contain beyond its own capaciousness." What I had perceived was somehow within me and part of me, and so threw my notion of myself into an open spectrum. Something was up. I felt I was waiting for the other shoe to drop.

One day it did, some three months or so after the insight of play. I received an anonymous letter, this time truly crank and strange, yet strangely accurate and straightforward. The writer pointed out that

I was being surrounded by a web of entanglements that would soon engulf me, that my real thrust was my spiritual longing, and that, unless my heart had totally hardened, I would recognize the truth of his words and immediately drop out of the world of affairs and pursue the true longing of my heart.

By then my seminars had grown in demand; spontaneous groups were forming to promote my child theory and were calling on me increasingly. I was asked if I would prepare a summary of my argument to present to the Senate committee in charge of the Department of Health, Education and Welfare; to the California senators considering a bill for early school enrollment, and so on—while invitations came from educational groups, colleges, and parent groups.

A battle ensued between my calculating brain and my longing heart. One day my heart won out. I drove the sixty miles to the home of my seminar director, burst into tears, resigned from the seminar-lecture circuit, left her with the job of processing herself out of a job, deprogramming coming events, and doing the best she could with the financial debacle. I gave my daughter (my remaining dependent) over to friends for safekeeping, and left, with no forwarding address. I fully expected never to see any of them, or be heard of, again. Had I not spent my publisher's advance for my child book, I would have scrapped it as well.

Leaving the world of seminars, lectures, applause, and criticism (and the first promise of serious money in my life) had been no sacrifice. The damage done in our "monstrous misunderstanding" of birth and child-rearing was a difficult emotional row to hoe. Far more critical for me, I had no answer to the tragedy at all. Because I had delineated the problem graphically, my audiences projected on me their hope for, and expectation of, deliverance. In this age of professionalism, they looked for the neat how-to formula usually sold after the diagnosis, and I had no formula at all. I knew, further, that only a new paradigm, some genius bursting full-force on the social scene, with lightning in his hands, could break the sodden mass of our heavily sedated, comfortably polluted self-destruction. The stage was filled with the blind leading the blind, the pathetic posturings of egos promising other egos a power the ego cannot conceive, generate, or possess. A constant merger of spiritual bankruptcies created the temporary illusion of solvency, for which I hadn't a nickel to invest.

It was some three years before the sequence of events spinning off from my play insight clarified for me. It takes power to understand, even recognize power. The fact that an indescribable bonding-power can be awakened in us is perhaps intelligible only to someone who has undergone such an experience and its aftermath, as topology may be intelligible only to an advanced mathematician. And to say that a transformation of one's life can begin just by looking at a person's picture and being irritated by the *eyes* strains credibility for even the most open-minded.

At any rate, I dropped out of the ordinary world into an extraordinary one. With no notion of what to expect, I drove some 1,500 miles to spend some six weeks with the author of the anonymous letter urging me to break with the world. It was the strangest encounter I have ever had and, seen in retrospect, a necessary preparatory step in the changes happening to me. My self-appointed mentor's sole intent was (rightly) to "knock the bottom out of my mind." He couldn't tolerate it the way it was, and, being of a somewhat violent nature, he did a fair job.

Surely my academic arrogance, intellectual snobbery, cultural chauvinism, and spiritual pride were dealt blows in those six weeks. My mentor had an eclectic spiritual discipline based on the Advaita Vedantas (an ancient Hindu philosophy), Sufism, Tibetan mysticism, and a strong bias toward Carlos Castaneda and American Indian shamanism. For days and weeks he pounded his synthesis into me, often skipping sleep and food in favor of his rather furious broadside against my "frightful ignorance."

A near knockout took place in an incredible four-hour encounter one night, alone at an ancient American Indian "power place" some 10,500 feet up in the Big Horn range of Wyoming. My adviser sent me on this several-hundred-mile trip to do a solitary all-night "vigil" there, and as Castaneda-like as it sounds, and at the risk of losing all credibility with the reader, I will relate it.

My first task, on arriving at the ancient site that evening, was to figure a way over or through the impenetrable barbed-wire enclosure the government had installed to keep tourists from carting the whole area away. I was then supposed to sit, all night, in the center of this circle of stones to receive a beneficial power supposedly residing there. The task of getting through or over the enclosure seemed impossible, however, and finally silly. I simply couldn't take the venture seriously, couldn't understand getting myself into such foolishness, and, though alone, I was a bit embarrassed.

So I gave up, unrolled my sleeping bag in the back of my station wagon, tailgate open, and thought to sleep there, next to the site. A mild breeze cropped up, however, and played around my ears, rather niggling down inside them, preventing sleep. I pulled a hooded sweat shirt on, in spite of the warm evening, but the breeze irritatingly snuck in through cracks. Finally I wrapped a blanket around my head, with an air hole for my nose, but the irritating breeze only grew worse, whipping harder into my ears.

Suddenly the wind exploded into hurricane force and blew me, bodily, out of the car. I thought this ridiculous and impossible, but grabbed hold of the bumper and held on, the situation now a waking nightmare. The nightmare became ridiculous as the wind pulled me, stretched me out like a rubber band, all the way over to the edge of the enormous precipice, some hundred feet away, with its drop of hundreds of feet straight down.

I knew rationally that the situation couldn't be physically real, since bodies don't stretch, that I had to be in an "astral" or subtle state. This cool observation helped nothing since the wind was whipping me up and down at the precipice edge, determined, it seemed, to pull me loose from that bumper. I had a momentary "visionary glimpse" of a newspaper filler-item captioned: "Tourist found dead at bottom of cliff at ancient Indian site." At which point the seriousness of my situation gripped me—how logical the event would seem to my survivors—and I began to pray, fervently, to every member of the heavenly hierarchy referred to in history.

After an interminable period of this, I suddenly snapped back, more or less, into my body, but only as a point of awareness about where my navel is. Above me were two huge thumpings which I eventually recognized as the ventricles of my heart, wildly fast and out of phase with each other. On either side of me were large squashy objects pumping feverishly (my adrenals, I somehow knew), while below me was a big, grapefruit-sized ball of agitation I later assumed was my Chi or Kath, considered by Eastern disciplines the center of our being. The whole show was out of synchrony and I felt I was witnessing my body tearing itself to pieces.

To stem the tide I thought of regular deep breathing, which helps stabilize the heart in tachycardia, but I had no connection with my body. I was an observer in it, not ruler of it. I couldn't find my head or my lungs. Only after intense effort did I make some connection and get some grip on my breath. It was weak, shallow stuff and responded slowly. Meanwhile I kept up a general running patter, praying for any help any handy deity might care to give me.

Eventually I regained enough control of my body to get under the steering wheel. Every breath and motion seemed a peculiar, slurry, weak, and vapid act, taking place through remote controls that connected poorly and demanded massive effort. As I got the car going and headed down the mountain, though, fragmentation began to dissipate. I felt more "solid" with each mile. Some twelve miles down I found a parking area, pulled over to sleep, and noticed that it was after two in the morning. My head was splitting and I was ill. I had first stretched out on my sleeping bag shortly after nine thirty, about four and a half hours before.

In addition to having sent me to my near-demise, my mentor introduced me, of all things, to what is called *Hamsa* meditation, and the *mantra* (a term which is discussed in Chapter XIII) *Om Namah Shivaya*. These were the core of his daily discipline, and just happened to be the heart of Swami Muktananda's daily practice as well. At first I had feigned a polite tolerance of these foreign notions. Following the Indian power-place fiasco, however, I could, as Castaneda might say, no longer guarantee myself my old consensus—nor any other. Surely a hole had been knocked in the bottom of my mind and this "Yoga" business slipped in easily enough and became increasingly important and productive.

My mentor couldn't tolerate me, even so, and I felt myself simply an object of his esoteric experimentation. On the other hand, I couldn't deceive myself and go back to lecturing, the blind leading the blind. The Indian power-spot venture had been the negative opposite of the life-giving play insight still fresh in my mind. I could attribute the play experience to my long work on the subject, but the power-spot affair left me no place to hide. (I still haven't quite pieced that one out.) My rationale was bankrupt. I finally knew just how thoroughly I knew nothing, and I quit.

I retreated to the Blue Ridge Mountains in central Virginia, where my friend, Robert Monroe (you should know his book, *Journeys Out of the Body,* Doubleday, 1971), kindly sold me a well-isolated parcel of land some two miles from the nearest road, telephone, or electric line. Here I built a house and, with my remaining family, settled down to a private quiet life of organic gardening and meditation.

A series of astonishing and rich meditation experiences took place over those three years. My knowing and understanding were enlarged; my mind was thoroughly plowed, harrowed, and readied for replanting. Early in 1979, the same persistent follower of Muktananda, the one who had sent me his picture, wrote yet again. She had just read my third book, *Magical Child,* and urged me again to go and meet her swami, Muktananda. He was, she told me, in this country for his third world tour. To help bridge the gap this time, she sent me some of his books, including *Play of Consciousness,* on the cover of which was that once-irritating picture. The circle was closing. This time I was open, more able to receive. After a slow and casual start, those books engrossed me, every line spoke to me, everything began to make sense.

One evening I was reading Muktananda's little book, *Siddha Meditations.* A powerful visionary insight unfolded before me, ecstatic surges of power carried me beyond myself, but this time *to* my Self, a part of me I had never so directly encountered before. This lightning bolt proved a point of no return. Blake said: "If a fool persists in his folly he will become wise." As a sufficiently persistent fool, I had at least the wisdom to suspend my folly long enough to go check out this man. If he could, apparently, wreak such happy havoc on my nervous system from a distance, what might direct contact hold in store?

II

The Genesis of Genius

I approached the Indian "holy man" with an openness that would have been difficult had my own inexplicable "power experiences" and three years of meditation not prepared the way. Even so, I found the trappings of Muktananda's environment, which he carries with him like a turtle shell, alien and esoteric. Few accommodations were made to ease a stranger across the cultural barriers. It was sink or swim from the beginning. The evening program, open to the public supposedly as an introductory bridge, proved a solid two and a half hours cross-legged on the floor endurance test, of Hindu rites and Sanskrit chants designed, it seemed to me, to separate the wheat from the chaff at the outset.

Muktananda seemed at one moment icy, hard, and remote; the next unbelievably warm and loving. Magnetism and charisma, the stock-in-trade of the public figure, are not applicable to him. There was, though, a breaking inside me, some snap of a high-tension defensive wire, and sense of impending recognition on approaching him. I am familiar enough with projection to realize my own needs were looking for a target, but an obvious power radiated from him in turn.

Muktananda's words seemed conventional enough in some ways,

radical and improbable in others. He reiterates, in dozens of ways, that: "God dwells within you as *You*. Worship your Self, honor your Self." Equally, he balances this with: "See God in each other. Welcome each other with love." This inner-outer command summarized his position and one is likely to ask: So what's new? Actually, "worshiping your Self" sounds strenuously heretical to Western ears, even as that capitalized Self begins to take on definition.

Ordinarily I would have been ill at ease over the naive, open, and unembellished truisms I heard, yet here the force seemed tied up in those phrases. Nothing else would have matched the charged atmosphere or strange setting, and over the following days the word *God* began to move from the realm of a slight cultural embarrassment and safe abstraction into a heady, overwhelming presence. The lifelong generalization grew specific; the abstract grew concrete. Deep within, the notion reeled about: "Good God! It might be true."

There are many kinds of genius, and genius is the issue here. There are people in the world who are simply plugged into a different circuitry, one at a radical remove from the ordinary. I knew a mathematical genius once and he was different. It wasn't just that he could do tricks in his field, his mind-set had been changed in some way (if only in relation *to* his field). That there can be spiritual genius, a mind-set at a radical discontinuity with the average, is not so farfetched. Spiritual geniuses arise, even in our country. I have known such a person. He remained largely anonymous, since he had no "lineage," or tradition as in India, but had emerged with abilities quite outside the ordinary and, wisely, cloaked those abilities carefully.

Like the insight-postulate, genius arrives full-blown in the brain, but only in a well-prepared one. The genius always goes beyond the outer limits of the known and possible. Genius is a created effect, drawn not from the commonsense world available to the ordinary, but from mind's imaginative creativity. Periodically, through the same insight function that brings us great art or discovery, a "postulate in person" arises, an absolute balance of mind/brain, body, world, and creation itself.

Genius appears from areas of intense social involvement along a particular line, just as the Eureka! insight results from a high level of passionate personal investment. The same processes are at work, the same format is followed, the same source is tapped.

An intense and prolonged activity, generated by a sufficient number of people along *any* specific line, will eventually produce its peak and even its genius. The postulate in person will arrive full-blown on that social scene. Bach, a fifth-generation musician in an era of intense musical activity, was such a product. But Bachs do not appear in Eskimo tribes. (Eskimos have their own art and genius.) A law of development is that like attracts like. A culture is like a person in that, "To him who has it is given; to him who has not, it's taken away—even that little he had."

Arthur Koestler and others point out that India is a tight-packed mass of nonsense, hysteria, superstition, religious mania, silliness, and squalor. What needs to be added is that India also represents ages of accumulated investment along the lines of her perennial, absorbing national interest, which is knowledge of the psyche and spirit (i.e., psychology and/or spirituality).

Three-quarters of a billion souls are massed into that subcontinent, with an estimated eight million of them at any one time directly involved in full-time spiritual pursuit: the swamis, sannyasis, mendicant monks, sadhus, renunciants, and general holy men. All of which, backed by the supportive enthusiasms of at least some remainders of that vast populace, results in a lot of energy concentrated on a single issue. No matter what the focal point, this much energy must, by the very nature of creative thought, produce accordingly. There arise in India periodic high peaks of output in keeping with the nature of that input. That is, spiritual geniuses appear regularly, generation by generation, and always have.

In India, the genius doesn't appear among the professors or philosophers of the universities, nor among the hoi polloi who hawk their wares before the tourists, research psychologists, or religious dilettantes seeking sensation. The genius crops up largely unsung and in remote places. Often he is known only to a few. He may choose anonymity and have to be sought out. Few of these geniuses feel impelled to teach. They simply want to be left alone to *be* the fantastic state of experience opened within them. Rarely is one appointed by his Guru to *be* a Guru (more on that term shortly), and only in the last hundred years have a few been directed to take Yoga to the West.

Meanwhile, as with any other activity on earth, along with the genius appears a host of near-misses, well-meaning but weaker talents, imitators, outright frauds, and scoundrels. These (perhaps the latter in particular) ape the graces of the genius and clamor about on the public scene, rather muddying the waters. All of this is part and parcel of the way any human activity functions. At best we have many fine technicians but few scientists; thousands of piano teachers and students, few Horowitzes or Rubinsteins; Einsteins arise from an army of able but lesser men, and so on. Thus, in some way, no shaggy swami of questionable repute, rushing over here to cash in on a good thing, is wasted. Like attracts like, false teachers trap false students, to each his own as time filters chaff from wheat.

So, among the tawdry and hilarious show of the Guru-of-the-Month Club's decade of display: child-gurus pushed into carnival prominence by zealous parents; ninety-day wonders from Brooklyn back from an excursion-rate trip to India as self-declared enlightened gurus seducing the throng of panting young things throwing flowers in their paths as they write books on cosmic orgasm; burned-out psychedelics shaving their heads and donning robes; stodgy pedants quoting dead Scripture while stuffing themselves on fried chicken; the real Guru just does his thing and bides his time.

Between the genius and the ordinary is a fundamental gap—of passion, esprit, daring; a certain ruthless tenacity and willingness to push beyond the known and risk one's very being. This discontinuity threatens us. We sense that the genius has powers of mind and character that we don't have, and his very presence behooves us to move beyond our ordinary self. This is why the genius is so often stoned by the populace. This is also why, without genius, we sink into lethargy and inertia.

The denial of genius is the denial of possibility beyond what we know and consider safe and acceptable. Our denial locks us into the confines of our fixed system. Back in the 1950's, I saw a corporation advertisement which boasted: "No genius here! Just solid technicians working together to solve the problems of science." I knew then that we were headed for trouble, a slow slide toward the idiot-end of the bell-curve graph. Only when our cultural model comes from outside the limits of the known and possible, that is, from genius, can our current system even maintain a middling average of sanity or stability.

Blake said: "He who calumniates great men calumniates God." Yet our pettiness continually prompts us to heap calumny on great men, lest we be challenged by them to bestir ourselves and emulate them. There is, as well, a chronic "academic stoning" of great men by small academic minds. (One thinks of Noam Chomsky, a veritable canon of a thinker, target of decades of peashooting academic jealousies; or so brilliant a person as Carlos Castaneda being "exposed" by petty nitpickers.)

Blake also observed that: "Genius can't exceed itself." There are no lesser or greater geniuses, nor is there any historical progression of genius. They don't quantitatively add to a pool that makes each greater. Genius is a mind open to a certain continuum of mental activity and either you are there or you aren't. This hardly means that all geniuses are alike. None of them are. All roads of genius do not lead to a genius-Rome.

With a spiritual genius there is the brass to "embezzle God's talents" (as Northrop Frye put it[1]), to plunge into an area of mind and experience considered sacrosanct, forbidden, or critically dangerous (perhaps for good reason), and the capacity to wrest from that realm the highest prize and bring that back as a boon to all who dare accept the gift. The genius of a particular art or profession seems called on to risk his professional life or image, but the spiritual genius risks his *very* life and structure of mind/brain. Just as a mathematical genius breaks into a realm where he interprets his reality mathematically and sees things in a unique way, so the spiritual genius breaks into a realm that encompasses the total capacity of mind/brain and creation. He can then range the whole continuum of experience. This is called "self-realization" because that continuum is found within the human mind/brain and (reportedly) is recognized as one's own, actual being, or Self. (The Australian Aborigine's Dream-Time incorporated some aspects of this capacity, which is obviously as old as mankind itself.)

The problem is, variations of even a minor sort can produce novel effects in our reality. A person can undergo extraordinary capacity-changes: a religious rebirth; synchronization of brain hemispheres opening some aspect of continuum consciousness; become able to "read minds"; pull nonordinary stunts, materialize objects or even move them without touching them; or even undergo actual "realization" in its Eastern sense—and still be completely unable to teach or guide another person. Yet the moment someone breaks through into some mental area outside the norm, he tends to cash in on it, rush out to the marketplace and set himself up as a big shot, a Guru.

Surely few terms are as sullied as *Guru*. The word is Sanskrit for dark-light. It stands for a function of development within us for moving, or maturing, from ignorance to knowledge, or from "darkness to light." The Latin word *educare,* from which we get education, meant essentially the same thing: leading forth into knowledge. Guru refers to a developmental process within us, and development of ability is the issue at stake.

The development referred to has a twofold aspect: *awakening* a particular natural potential in us (which is always the first task of a teacher), and *guiding* us in the development of that potential (the ongoing aspect of any teacher or teaching).

The difference between Muktananda and an ordinary teacher, or between his Siddha Yoga and any other teaching, is the potential which is awakened and developed. Muktananda is called a *Siddha* because he carries on an exceedingly old and unbroken line of teachers who, through hard work and discipline, developed the maximum potential of the mind/brain. And nothing less than this ultimate, this universality, is the potential which Muktananda evokes in others, and which he guides through ongoing development.

This potential which the Siddha can awaken in another is an inner power that, like any other potential, lies dormant *until* awakened. And it can only be awakened by one who has been not only so awakened (which is comparatively simple since so natural to us), but has developed the power involved (which is a bit more of an accomplishment). The power is called *Shakti,* the process of awakening is called *Shaktipat,* and the awakening is almost useless, in fact, it can dissipate, unless there is then an ongoing guidance, or Yoga, to develop the power.

Anyone with good intent and some intelligence can become a teacher. But one doesn't *become* a Guru. One is chosen to be a Guru by a Guru. (This, unfortunately, is a very rare event. There are probably less than half a dozen of them in the world at any one time.) The simplest test of a Guru is the most direct: *Can* he awaken one's personal power, that is, deliver Shaktipat, and then guide that awakened power in its development? The student or disciple is the criterion, the yardstick: Does he undergo transformation that specifically changes his relations with this world for the better?

Three short paragraphs concerning Muktananda's history will suffice: he left home at fifteen without a cent or backward glance, knowing exactly what he was going to do. He spent twenty-five years of intense personal discipline and study in all branches of Yoga, or spiritual discipline. By age forty, he was a "successful" Yogi, with national fame and the appropriate following. And a gnawing discontent, for he knew that he was not complete. He was led to Nityananda, one of the most obscure, strange, but apparently powerful yogis of history. And, at forty, an age when such is difficult for the male animal (particularly for an utterly confident—and contemptuous of incompetence—proud, arrogant, headstrong, egotistical, and truly intelligent person as Muktananda was), he switched his life-role, became the disciple again, submitted himself completely to Nityananda, and made a second radical break with life as he had known it.

For nine years Muktananda struggled, in solitude, with the inner battle of transformation Nityananda set for him. Every few years he would return, only to be dismissed at a glance by Nityananda, as "half-baked, unfinished." The struggle of those years is a classic of the harrowing, often frightful and dangerous journey within, as a brain's entire conceptual process undergoes reorganization; a willful collapse into chaos out of which a radically different process of mind can emerge. I refer in the Notes to the fact that Muktananda's body changed radically, too, as had happened to all the Siddhas.[2]

The result of these nine years was not just enlightenment in its

classical sense, but, far more, the ability to deliver Shaktipat, the
ability to literally just reach out and touch someone (or even think
about them, speak to them) and awaken personal power within
them. Shaktipat was apparently Nityananda's goal for Muktananda, and, eventually, before his death in 1961, Nityananda passed
on to Muktananda his power, his "office" as Guru, the practice of
Siddha Yoga (the discipline of the age-old lineage of "perfected
masters"), and the command to take Shaktipat and Siddha Yoga to
the world.

The issue of Muktananda's genius is the issue of Shaktipat.
Siddha Yoga itself has been called "whatever happens around
Muktananda" and is peculiarly hard to define since it continually
redefines itself. In fact, it defines itself around the particular individual involved. Siddha Yoga is an example of a fixed goal and
highly flexible plan for getting to that goal. The goal is realization of
one's inner Self, which means one's own, unique unity with the
creative process. The plan is anything and everything necessary to
that particular person for getting to that goal. The goal is absolutely
within one's mind, so the way for getting there also comes from
within, and Muktananda is the catalyst bringing the development
about.

Meditation is the term used for this Yoga, although chanting out-
weighs actual sitting-still meditation in practice. And Shakti is the
power always at stake. Since Shakti is a personal-universal energy,
Muktananda's Siddha Yoga is more a *tantra*, a generative force,
than a Yoga in its classical sense. Muktananda continually links
everything he does with ancient Scripture out of his background
and lineage, but what is actually unfolding around him may be
quite unique in history. The Yoga or discipline involved with Muktananda is not a way of eventually awakening or developing some
personal power, but a critical way of dealing with and controlling a
power which almost immediately manifests from within a person
coming into contact with Muktananda.

Leonard Smith, a young heart surgeon from Gainesville, Florida,
was disturbed over a tendency toward emotional hardness in his
profession, brought on by the continual exposure to death. He took
up meditation as a possible means to maintain some openness and

empathy with his patients. Eventually he was led to meet Baba Muktananda. During an intensive (an initiation into Siddha meditation) in August of 1979, Smith reports:

"Baba grabbed me by the bridge of the nose and held on. I seemed to sense him saying 'Stop thinking and just experience this.' I saw blue electricity going from Baba's arm up to his head, and then saw my own Self as a body of blue energy."

Leonard's rational, academic mind resisted strenuously at this point, with the usual arguments about illusion, hypnotism, and such. Then he saw his right arm, transparent blue, with every tissue, nerve, and blood vessel visible, ". . . clinging to the branch of a tree, holding on." (This was a graphic demonstration of one's academic ego holding on to its position of dominance.) "I felt each finger being pried loose, one at a time, until suddenly I snapped, like a rubber band, into Baba's head. There I found myself in an immense vacuum—an infinite space. A wave of emotion swept up from my belly and I wept for fifteen minutes or more."

This was, Smith said, ". . . an archetypal weeping"—he wept for all the suffering and death in the world. He was ". . . cleaned out, left calm and peaceful" afterward. His life changed markedly from that moment. He became centered, calm, full of love and empathy for his patients, continually more skilled at his profession, a source of strength for those around him. (And he returns at every opportunity to continue his ongoing relationship with Baba.)

Smith's story is a classical account of Shaktipat, a personal power so unknown in the West, sapped as we are by our technology, that a credibility gap looms. The new holonomic theory by physicist David Bohm offers a splendid model of this power, and since genius brings us that which is beyond the outer limits of our known, we need all the help we can get.

Shakti is the bonding-power which holds things together. The Guru *is* this bond of power and its development in us. We have, in this century, monkeyed around with some of the outward, physical manifestations of the bond, as it holds physical matter together. To balance things and survive our tampering, we need to turn to the inner form.

I recall as a youngster hearing, with awe, that a single lump of coal contained enough energy to run a steamship for a year, were atomic energy to be tapped. In 1956, David Bohm proposed that if we compute the "zero quantum energy in a single cubic centimeter of empty space" (which is about next to nothing at all), we would come up with 10^{38} ergs, the explosive power of roughly ten billion *tons* of uranium fission. Bohm spoke of that vast energy in a speck of nothing as "currently unavailable," but, in his youthful optimism, assumed that eventually we would tap into it.

Unlocking the comparatively small energy in the atom has cast a pall of gloom over our world. We might think, God help us, should Bohm's early proposal bear fruit. Judging from Bohm's thought in the last few years, however, I think he may have intuitively touched on the realm of Shakti back then, that is, power as itself.

I once envisioned a radical mathematics unlocking Bohm's 10^{38} ergs. I know now that an equally radical turning within is what is involved. The power of the Guru which can bind the scattered fragments of our life into unity is the issue. If the split atom has cast a pall of gloom over our world, the awakened Shakti within dispels that gloom. Shakti is the energy of creation itself. Allowed to develop within, this energy always moves for unity, it can order into coherence our mind/brain split asunder by the force of madness about us, and bring us into balance with this awesome universe we carry within our skulls.

III

The Order of Things

David Bohm's new paradigm for physics offers a splendid model for explaining personal power and Shaktipat. Bohm's model fits the ancient theories of Siddha psychology with fine precision and marks a significant link between Western science and Eastern spirituality.[1]

The problem facing physics today is that there are no particles, no basic building blocks of matter as always presumed. All that can be found is an underlying vibratory energy. Matter manifests, Bohm proposes, through the interweaving of different energy vibrations. Bohm calls the vibratory energy out of which this interweaving manifests the *implicate order,* since all possibilities are implied within it. Bohm calls that which is manifest out of this energy (the physical universe) the *explicate order,* that which is made explicit.

Anything manifested in the explicate order is *enfolded* in the implicate order. By "enfolded" Bohm means that anything in the physical universe exists within the energy of the implicate order in a potential state, rather as a tendency toward expression.

For instance, consider the way insight breaks into the brain: Kekulé's theory of the benzine ring appeared to him first as a ring of snakes in a particular formation. We speak of this as symbolic of the eventual benzene ring. We could say that the benzene ring and the entire world of chemicals resulting was implied in Kekulé's dream. His vision, then, was the medium between the implicate order and the eventual explicate order of actual, man-made, and manipulated chemicals.

Mozart's initial perception of a symphony as an instant's gestalt was the transition between the implicate order's possibility and the explicate order's pages of musical manuscript which could be interpreted by others and turned into music. The symphony was enfolded within the implicate order and unfolded in time and space in the concert hall. When my pianist friend perceived the entire sonata, he had experienced it as a kind of musical grace, an insight arriving full-blown in the brain, perhaps as originally conceived by Mozart, enfolded within the implicate order awaiting its unfolding in time.

The difficult part of Bohm's theory for us Westerners, and its direct correspondence with Eastern thought, is that the implicate order is *consciousness*. The energy out of which anything and everything is made is conscious energy, which, of course, calls for a redefinition of consciousness. Any definition we attempt to make of this power is, however, of necessity drawn from our physical world. And the physical world, or explicate order, is of a different order of energy and so its terminology doesn't fit.

The power of consciousness, or the implicate order, is far greater than the power of the explicate order; far greater than *any* explicit manifestation made out of that great energy. All physical matter is of an essentially weak construction, undergoing a constant process of dissolution and rebuilding. Yet at the heart of matter is an incalculable power, as witness the release of energy in atomic fission.

The entire physical world, with its time and space, results from impulses which manifest by complex mathematical relations of frequencies within the implicate order. The explicate expression can be thought of as an order arising out of chaos through relating frequencies of energy. The chaos is the as-yet-unformed energy of the implicate order. This chaos is not a disorder or confusion but a very orderly potential, perhaps like a steady state of undifferentiated frequency.

The explicate order, the whole physical universe, is only a "ripple" on the surface of consciousness, and beyond the implicate order itself, according to Bohm, lie vaster fields of even more powerful energies. At the core of it all is what Bohm calls the realm of insight-intelligence, which I take to be the source of creativity, where the postulate comes from.

When we use words like *beyond, bigger, at the core of, on the surface of,* and so on, we are using explicate terms which can't be applied to the implicate or insight realms. We have to represent it somehow, though, and have only "explicate terms" at our disposal. But *parts* indicate a thingness or concreteness which is misleading. The implicate and insight realms are states, not places. Location can be drawn from them, but they have no location. Time and space can't be applied to them but can be expressed out of them. No energy has time, space, or location, though time, space, and location can be effects of energy.

Bohm uses the word *holomovement* for this creative system of insight, implicate and explicate orders of energy. The holomovement is a single unit, a gestalt, an impulse or state which cannot be divided in any way but which can be represented in an infinite number of ways. Everything within the holomovement is enfolded within itself, within its single energy or state. And the same goes for any of its expressions. The entire explicate order is enfolded within itself. All time is enfolded in any second; all matter within any bit of matter; all consciousness within any single mind/brain; all conceivable space within any particle of space.

The universe operates like a hologram where any piece contains the information of the whole. Reality takes place through a kind of projecting out from each of the apparent parts to the whole, to each other, the whole to the parts, and so on, creating in effect a three-dimensional space of time and events. This is something the poets and saints have always claimed, as witness Blake's most famous quatrain:

> *To see a World in a Grain of Sand*
> *And a Heaven in a Wild Flower,*
> *Hold Infinity in the palm of your hand*
> *And Eternity in an hour.*

Stanford University's neuropsychologist, Karl Pribram, uses the holonomic theory to account for current problems of brain research. He speaks of the brain mathematically constructing "hard reality by interpreting frequencies from a dimension transcending time and space." Pribram assumes that the brain couldn't operate as a hologram unless it were part of a larger hologram. Reality takes place through a brain hologram projecting out its implied view toward a whole, the whole toward its parts, and so on.

Pribram thinks each organism represents in some manner the universe, and, conversely, each portion of the universe represents the organisms within it. Perception can't be understood without an understanding of the nature of the physical universe and the nature of that universe can't be understood without an understanding of the observing perceptual process.

The brain of any organism constructs its reality as an explicate set of organized and clarified frequencies from the implied order. The fundamental question is: whether our mind is an "emergent property" of the brain, simply an effect of our interaction with our environment; or whether the mind reflects the basic organization of the universe, including our own brain. Pribram believes that our perceptual response is between the brain as a hologram and the larger hologram of which it is both part and also at least a "spokesman for the whole."

This idea that the brain is a hologram of a larger hologram which extends to the whole universe might, conceivably, be accepted someday by our current brand of academic-scientific consensus thinking. But Bohm's holomovement goes as far beyond such a universal hologram-brain notion as that goes beyond our current notion of a self-encapsulated little brain registering a vast outer world. According to Bohm's theory our mental reservoir is such that the physical universe is but the "merest ripple" on our actual surface, which is the holomovement. The holomovement's mode of being is through the energy of consciousness and all this is, of logical necessity, inherent within the domain of our brain.

The word *brain,* by itself, is where an insufficiency lies, however, for the brain is an explicate-order arrangement, which, by definition, is too weak an energy system for anything beyond explicate-order energy interaction. So we can't say, or imply, that the brain encompasses, as though it owns, the holomovement. Perhaps the holomovement is implied in, or enfolded within the brain, but it can't be manifest there. That which is manifest is automatically of the explicate order, a shift of modality.

The brain, however, is the physical manifestation of the holomovement, and so, like its own hologram, the universe, the brain is but the merest ripple on the surface of consciousness, or the implicate order. The term mind/brain allows us to think of the brain realistically. The brain must be seen as an instrument of mind, just as the body is an instrument of the brain. The mind, then, is the holomovement as implied within the brain, but not manifest. Which is to say, the mind is not part of or in physical reality. The *brain* is the way the mind *is* in physical reality. The mind is not "real" in the same sense the brain is real, when reality is considered that which is physical or in the explicate order. To be in physical reality requires an explicate mode of being, and that mode, for the mind, is the brain. The mode of being is the way of instrumentation, and an instrument is always in service. Brain, then, is in service of the mind. Mind can't be in physical reality except as a brain, but brain is only a weak-energy expression of something, and that something is the mind, which is always of the implicate and insight orders of energy, an issue that will occupy Chapter IV.

Insight, as discussed earlier, is creative thought which arrives full-blown in, rather than being thought by, the brain. Insight is expressed through the power of consciousness (which in this sense is itself but an instrument of insight). Insight, since of a vastly greater energy, can influence thought, shape it, and keep it coherent. In order to be intelligent and express insight, thought must be open to the power of consciousness and be capable of being *used* as an instrument of insight. No thought is possible except through the power of consciousness, but a certain amount of this energy is inherent within brain construction and the whole explicate order. And, sadly, this energy can be employed in isolation from insight-intelligence.

The biological plan built into our genes is for development of thought as that instrument of insight. This development is, genetically, an orderly, logical, and thorough design. In actuality, in practice, it fails miserably (for reasons I will touch on later, and explored rather thoroughly in *Magical Child*). Thought doesn't develop as the instrument of insight-intelligence, and so never has the full and enormous power of consciousness available.

The child is in consciousness. Discursive thought and verbal logic don't begin until around age seven and take several years to develop to full dominance in our brain. But the child is not, as a result, closer to *insight* than the adult. The child may be closer to intelligence, but insight, as an order of creation, must use thought, if it is to be expressed in the world, just as it must use consciousness. Which is to say, thought is designed as the explicate order of insight-intelligence, or, brain is designed as the instrument of mind.

All of this is developmental, however, not preset or ordained in some divine hierarchy other than the functions through which the system operates. The body is an instrument of the brain and develops in very clear-cut, logical stages according to the needs of that brain. The brain is an instrument of mind and develops in very clear-cut, logical stages according to the needs of that mind. The whole issue of human development is that thought must first be developed in order to be an instrument for creative insight and in order to utilize the power of consciousness.

Intelligence is the ability to interact, the ability to respond successfully to the interweaving of energies or patterns of consciousness through which the holomovement expresses itself. Intelligence may or may not use thinking as an instrument of that interaction. (And, needless to say, not all thinking is intelligent.) Animals show intelligence in their ability to interact and this certainly uses a form of thinking, independent mental activity such as problem-solving and decision-making. Plants exhibit intelligence in making adaptive changes to their environment. Intelligence is the pattern of relationship that consciousness makes, and plants and animals are intelligent as needed, and conscious of necessity, since all energy configurations are made of consciousness. But thought, as a creative system, using *words* and verbal logic, seems distinctly human, and we need to clearly distinguish that thinking and consciousness are not the same.

Our problem is that thought takes over, as Bohm puts it, and becomes self-generative. By self-generative is meant a kind of closed-circuit, tape-looped effect of the brain, wherein the brain feeds on its own output, so to speak, rather than on insight-intelligence. Through enculturation and its resulting anxiety, thought relates exclusively to the brain, the body, and the outer world, and loses its connection with consciousness and insight. This is the case even though thought is itself only a form of consciousness, and without that power there could be no thought. But thought is a weak form of explicate energy which, isolated from the implicate order, is powerless to create, on the one hand, and powerless to interpret its domain correctly, on the other hand.

Thought can make minor manipulations of its explicate order, and can make things out of things already created, but it can't create, and it can't correct its own disorders. The only creativity available to isolated thought (aside from mathematics and the arts) occurs in connection with the Eureka! discoveries and insight-postulates discussed earlier. Aside from such novel incursions into thought from the powerful insight realm, brought about through passionate tenacity, thought can only reproduce itself or its products.

Thought becomes "self-moving," according to Bohm. Thought forms a world of its own in which it is everything, even though it is but a tiny manifestation, the least surface ripple on the implicate order of consciousness.

The world of its own which thought creates is the split-off world of the social-ego, a thought-construction isolated from general consciousness and so devoid of power. Self-generative thought does seem an emergent of brain alone, of the weak explicate order of energy which can't change anything, including itself. This kind of thought identifies with the explicate order, with the brain, body, and physical world, and of necessity, since it is functionally and perceptually isolated from the holonomic movement (though this separation is, in the last analysis, illusory).

Bohm distinguishes, then, two kinds of thought: the one we generate with our own brain and the one generated by a "deeper mind" and given to us, that is, insight-intelligence. Only thought which results from alignment with the holonomic movement can itself be orderly, and creative. (Order is creation.) The very nature of our brain-generated thought produces a disorder because it identifies with and draws on only part of the system. Its frequencies are self-relating only and so give the impression of actuality, truth, or wholeness. But, leaving out the rest of the system, such thought is dis-harmonious, in discord with the smooth interactions of the system. So anything we do with this fragmented order of thinking is always out of balance and proves eventually destructive. This very disorder, in turn, blocks us from participating in the larger field of possible thought always available through insight-intelligence. Disorder and order can't coexist. Their waves don't cohere.

Self-generative thought, the semantic fabrications of the isolated social-ego, is *autistic* in the original sense of that term: thought that relates only to itself largely because it is unable to relate on a wider frequency. Autistic thinking in this sense is an inner, tape-looped circuitry verifying and feeding back on its own circuit while ignoring (because unable to compute) what is taking place outside the tight confines of its own definition.

Consider a room full of people, all aware of each other, communicating and making intelligent adjustment-responses; "relating frequencies" on a wide and smoothly efficient level. The autistic person sits in the midst of this intelligence *without* relating; without communication or cooperation; he shuts out (because unable to comprehend) the most common sensory information, and has only his closed world of his own making. He is limited to whatever frequency he can either generate within or manage to bring in through his faulty system. He sits in his powerlessness, unable to cope or interact, shut off from a vast possibility of which he can never, from his crippled state, know. And this "autistic" person is the social-ego and its encapsulated, semantic world, when seen from the standpoint of the holonomic movement.

Functionally isolated from the power and possibility of the rest of the system, thought can never take into account the infinite variables within the holomovement. Thus every move thought makes proves susceptible to contradiction at some point, and subject to disruption sooner or later. So this isolated thought develops a passion for prediction and control, trying, within the confines of its own weak and narrow limits, to fathom and "outthink" what always amounts to nothing less than the holonomic order itself. A semantic world of chaos and confusion is the only possible result.

Only insight-intelligence and the "high energy" of consciousness can order the limited and disorderly field of our thought into coherence and rapport with the holonomic order, according to Bohm. Insight can act by a direct wave-interference on the brain at the manifest level. This interference can change that brain and make it orderly.

Insight, according to Bohm, is the agent of change, an ". . . active intelligence that doesn't pay any attention to thought . . . [which] bypasses thought as of little importance." Insight removes all the blocks and confusions in thought; rearranges the very structural matter of the brain which underlies thought. Bohm says insight can remove that message which is causing confusion, leave the necessary information there, and leave that brain open to perceive reality in a different way.

Insight, then, offers far more than a rare flash of lightning imparting a new idea into the brain. It can be remedial, if allowed. For instance, Jane Ferrar, then teaching sociology at New York University, met Muktananda in 1974, received his mantra, *Guru Om,* and attended a few meditation sessions. She felt that nothing much had happened. One hot, April afternoon she was riding the subway to her class. She was unprepared, late, harassed, and kept dropping papers and books. ". . . All of a sudden, out of nowhere," she reports, "a voice began to roar around in a circle in the top of my head: 'Guru Om, Guru Om,' as though it were circling, at great speed, inside a bright neon tube . . . then the roaring went down to my heart and began to turn over and over gently in time to my heartbeat. After a minute or two it charged back up to my head again, then swooped back down to my heart. . . . It took all my attention and forced me to focus on the rhythm lolling in my heart. But then my mind would begin to chatter and 'Guru Om' would rush back up to my head and roar around, wiping out the resistance. 'You're going crazy,' my mind finally informed me, 'right here on the Seventh Avenue subway you are having a psychotic episode.' But Guru Om rushed up to my head and absorbed the thoughts once again. . . . It wiped out the irrelevancies and cleared the space for full concentration. . . . I taught a wonderful class that day. . . . The experience never left me . . . my life was transformed."

Our ordinary thought is a "gross" product of the brain which can't produce other than its own gross products. So thought can't change the gross level or nature of its own brain and production any more than hamburger coming out of the grinder could turn around and change that grinder. A person's way of thinking, his brain program shaped since birth, can never change through its own actions. Self-generated thought can only reproduce itself, though it continually changes the guises of that self-production to imply novelty. Self-moving thought is always self-incriminating, tangling in its own web of rationale.

This is what makes our life so infernally frustrating. We have, apparently, only our thought as our tool for getting along. And all of our thought, our "understanding," comprehension, plans, hopes, schemes, maneuvers, and "progress" seem, sooner or later, to turn to dust and ashes. Our "only tool" fails us constantly. Our answer has been to band together with others, and work for a consensus of opinion about our plight. We think that if we group enough isolated thought together we will produce a workable and whole unit. This is like expecting a sufficient quantity of negative numbers to fuse into a positive set.

What needs exploration here is the relation of thought, consciousness, and insight. Surely, as Bohm claims, "Thought trying to go beyond its place blocks what is beyond"—but what *is* thought's place? What is its role? Often philosophies and theories, particularly Eastern ones, begin to look on thinking as the universal culprit, as a vast error of nature, perhaps. But nothing in our natural endowment is error, and to miss the role of thought is to miss the nature of human development.

Generated mostly by the brain, equated with the isolated, fragmented, and anxiety-ridden ego, dissociated from the coherency and energy of the whole, our thought is nevertheless the vehicle of creative imagination. Surely thought in its undeveloped and undisciplined state, given to gibberish and foolishness as it is, and locked into compulsive roof-brain chatter, blocks that which is beyond. But this has nothing to do with its potential or what nature intended for it.

Thought, consciousness, and insight form a trinity, one which can't, in the final analysis, be divided. Thought is *man;* insight is *God;* consciousness is the bonding-power, the connecting force, the Holy Spirit, that Shakti or energy which underlies all reality. The issue is, what brings about insight, or what is our relation with God? What are the antecedents by which the postulate arrives full-blown in the brain, for instance, bringing that transforming power? The postulate arrives in that brain which has asked that kind of question; which is capable of receiving that particular insight-answer; and which is capable of being transformed as needed to translate that insight into the common domain of the explicate order. And, asking the question, receiving the answer, and translating it all involve thought.

A great answer is no answer to a person who has not asked that question, or thought along those lines. Had Kekulé's ring of snakes appeared to a painter or musician we may have had something other than a benzene ring. Were insight to break into an unprepared or weak mind/brain, no reordering would take place and no translation into the common domain would be given. Outside the phenomenon of Shaktipat, there are no cases of insight-revelation of any stature taking place without proper preparation simply because the law of development precludes such a possibility. The proper preparation involves thought, and the nature of the inputs of thought enters into the nature of the insight achieved. Our general receptivity enters into the nature of what we receive.

Earlier I outlined the fourfold process which gives insight: the postulate, scientific discovery, spiritual conversion, and so on. Throughout this process, right up to its final cessation for the revelation itself, thought predominates. The period of gathering the materials can last for years; thought must discriminate continually as to the choice of those materials. That choice is critical since the end-product, while giving a whole greater than the sum of its parts, is nevertheless subject to the nature of those parts. Even the intensity of purpose, which is our will, and our power, centers around thought. And when the materials of the search "take over" and dictate their own ends, they do so through the medium of thought, and it is thought that must undertake those ends. When the person must serve the truth given in the revelation, devote himself to the translation of his gift into the common domain, thought is the instrument of that service.

An enormous amount of thinking must take place before any suspension of thinking will give creative insight-discovery. Mere suspension of thought doesn't necessarily result in insight. A medical man designed a system of stress-reduction which involved total muscular relaxation. The system was difficult to master, but those succeeding found that when truly relaxed, they couldn't think. (This is because ordinary thinking is verbal; words are constructed originally through muscular activity, and the link between muscle and word is never broken on primary levels.) Their suspension of thinking did not usher in revelation, however, since creativity responds *to* the products of thought.

An exception to the preparatory period of thinking seems to be found in *grace*—insight or beneficial events that seem freely given, not of our making and not clearly deserved. Even here connecting links can be found. A split system is always seeking wholeness, just as a newborn infant is automatically expecting and primed for appropriate responses. A devotee of Muktananda's, for instance, was hospitalized in Melbourne, Australia. The devotee's nurse, Ellen Gillanders, complained of funny rushes up her spine when she went into his room, and occasionally felt something sitting on the back of her neck when she went in. She had trouble with her balance in the room and had to hold onto the furniture. Her patient gave her one of Baba's mantra cards. She glanced at Baba's picture on the card and began reading.

As she did so, her feet rooted to the floor, her body began swaying in huge, gravity-defying circles. Nurse Gillanders panicked. She staggered to the bedside table, thrust the mantra card down emphatically, with her right hand, and turned to leave such crazy business. As she did so, her left hand picked up the card and refused to let go. In serious confusion, she stopped still, grew quiet, looked at her patient, and asked what was up. He talked with her briefly about Muktananda and suggested she visit the Melbourne ashram. She did, and has been a Siddha student of meditation ever since.

Nurse Gillanders's logical, rational side thrust the card away, but her intuitive, holistic side knew better, picked it up and wouldn't let go. Surface thought is not the whole of our being, and our whole being is constantly striving for reunification.

Surely the role of thought must be fully evaluated, lest we miss the point of discipline and development *of* thought. Part of the strength of Siddha meditation and Baba's approach lies in its three-fold design: he gives grace, insight which, because of its power, can shift our orientation and open us to learning and gaining further insight; he gives instruction and insists we learn, which strengthens our new orientation through organizing our thinking; and he teaches meditation, which aligns our system with the holonomic order and maintains that alignment.

A satisfactory why-ness for our life, so often lacking, is found in Siddha Yoga because it incorporates the threefold life pattern: thought is our ordinary ego-self; consciousness is our Shakti within us and the Guru without who stands as model, the bonding-power from which our life arises and which holds all together in unity; and insight-intelligence is our very Self, the totality of our being.

Muktananda sees the world as a product of love and joy, a great explosion of creative energy, an exuberance he displays with each breath and which we find, through his modeling, equally in our-selves. The spiritual being is not some vapid, fey, otherworldly wraith, as anyone meeting seventy-two-year-old Muktananda (and trying to keep up with him) quickly finds out. The spiritual being is an integrated whole person of thought, resting in the power of con-sciousness, open to insight-intelligence.

So the answer for our anxiety-ridden and crippled thought is not to escape the world or try to shut it out, but to see it for what it really is, invest in our seeing, and be what we are designed to be. The only way to be as designed is to get into and remain in align-ment with the function of creativity, the instant-by-instant creation of our universe. Then our thought, personality, and life have the power of the universe behind them.

IV

Instruments of Mind

The words *mind* and *brain* are often used interchangeably and the results are confusing. Body is an instrument of brain; brain is an instrument of mind; mind can be considered an instrument of consciousness which, in this sense can be considered an instrument of insight-intelligence. Certainly body and brain are a unit, brain isn't much good without body, but if we are going to use the word brain we clearly don't mean the pancreas or liver. The same distinction must be held for mind and brain.

The late Wilder Penfield, one of our century's great brain surgeons and research persons, offered a distinction between mind and brain (an offering rather rigorously turned down by our current biologists and brain researchers). In his long career, Penfield removed the skulls and probed the brains of some fifteen hundred people. Since the brain has no feeling, only a local anesthetic is needed to open the skull. The patient is then conscious and responsive.

Penfield's operations often lasted for hours, as he took advantage of this open-skulled opportunity to explore. He found certain tiny areas of the brain which, when electrically stimulated, gave the patient a full, five-sensory replay of some event in the patient's past (say, for instance, falling off a haystack in grandfather's barn at age seven). So long as the spot was stimulated, the event would run its course and stop. Restimulated, the event would repeat. Remove the stimulation in midstream and the event stopped; restimulated, it started over again. (While only a tiny spot elicited this particular replay, large areas of the brain took part, as with all brain activity.)

The patient would report the replayed event to Penfield as it took place. Yet the patient was open-eyed, looking at Penfield as he did so. Two distinctly different reality-events were taking place at the same time for him and the patient reported the two as equal, though his logic ruled that he had to be "just remembering" the barn incident. "But," Penfield would ask, "where are *you* that you witness two separate but equal events?" The patient would reply: "Just watching both."

From many such cases Penfield concluded that mind and brain are separate entities; that mind perceives the brain's perceptual functions but is not the result of those functions; that mind has no memory or content, that brain furnishes those on demand or as needed; that mind "runs," and in turn draws its sustenance from, the brain. Penfield mused that if we could ever prove that mind could under any circumstance receive its energy from any source other than the brain, we would know that "immortality" was functionally possible.

Where Penfield erred was in assuming that mind received its energy from the brain. The opposite is the actual case, though *mind* then proves a bit more than just some passive recipient. Mind is obviously the personal awareness that perceives, and evidence for this awareness receiving its energy from a source *other* than brain has been around for some time.

Brain-wave (EEG) tracings of Yogis and Zen masters show that these disciplined people can shut off all sensory response from their brains. They withdraw from their own brain and a gun can be fired six inches from their ear and the EEG detects no physiological response. There is no way this can be faked nor can it be done through some stoic control. To overcome brain function requires a force stronger than those functions themselves. The brain can no more "shut itself down" than the average person can suspend roof-brain chatter.

These people are not unconscious at the time of their withdrawal from their brain. They are, if anything, more conscious than ever. Sensory awareness and consciousness are not identical. These people's minds are still quite functional though withdrawn from bodily sensory activity. They willfully withdraw consciousness from the brain, at which point that brain is no longer active except in autonomic body maintenance.

Consciousness is not an emergent of the brain, but that force which powers the brain. Even bodily awareness and ordinary verbal thought are "emergents" of the brain only because they are consciousness as processed through its instrument *of* brain.

One of the most significant but ignored facts from brain research is that researchers can't find where in the brain perception occurs. The whole fallacy of mind as an emergent of brain breaks down in light of this fact, so the fact is simply ignored.

David Bohm spoke of the physical world, the implicate order supporting it, "vaster energies" beyond, and a final core of insight-intelligence. For untold centuries Siddha psychologists, the "realized beings" or geniuses of the East, have spoken of the holonomic movement in terms of "bodies." For each of us the holonomic movement unfolds and functions as our own personal being, so this personal terminology is both accurate and reasonable. The realized beings explore the nature of mind and reality by disciplining their unruly thought and entering into consciousness itself, and the striking thing about meditation is the unanimity of opinion about the resulting experience. The one unanimous agreement is that consciousness and the universe are of the same substance, all is mental experience. Yogic psychology speaks of four bodies: first, the *physical* body, its brain and its world-out-there. This is the explicate order, of course. Next comes the *subtle* body, which is the same as, or partakes of, Bohm's implicate order. Next is the *causal* body, which is the realm of potential without even "implications" of any manifestation in it; and finally comes the *supercausal* body, which is the witness of all states, the final core of awareness, the final "perceiver" of perceptions. The causal body or state is what Bohm referred to as "vaster energies beyond the implicate," and the supercausal is the realm of insight-intelligence, from which the postulate-revelation and all creation springs. This last state is without attributes or impingements on it from anything of which it is aware, and is the goal of the practice of *choiceless awareness,* of which Krishnamurti speaks, and is, of course, the *Self* in Siddha Yoga terms.

Robert Monroe has given us an articulate account of certain subtle body experiences in his book, *Journeys Out of the Body* (covers only a part of the vast experiences he had over a number of years). His institute in Faber, Virginia, has developed electronic processes to stimulate various kinds of subtle, perhaps causal, functions.[1] In my first encounter with one of his early ventures in 1975, I fell into a free state doing barrel rolls in space.

Kathy McCormick, former Spanish professor at San Jose State University, received Shaktipat from Muktananda, took a trip to India to visit his ashram there, and returned to her teaching. Meditating one day, she felt "the substance of her life collecting from all parts of her body." She became central in her body and then went out through the top of her head, "like a smoke." "Everything I thought of as myself, including my thinking, was there, except my physical body.

"I became too fascinated with the state and broke its concentration," she goes on, "and felt myself go back in through the top of my head, down the central channel, and spread out again into my body." She knew after this that she was somehow not her body. Eventually she returned to India and became a swami, or monk, in Muktananda's service.

Roy Mason, a pharmacist from Westchester County, New York, was visiting Baba in Miami Beach in February of 1980. It was a dark, rainy day when, after lunch, he sat down to meditate using the *Hamsa* mantra. Suddenly he felt his self being pulled out of every cell of his body "like an intermeshed Velcro fastener separating from each pore." He gathered speed, popped out of the top of his head, and burst through the window. Outside, he was astonished to see that everything was a brilliant light (he knew it was raining) and that he was himself a part of every particle of that light.

He pervaded everything, in fact, and was allowed to remain there for quite a while before returning to his body in the same manner he had left it.

According to yogic theory, the brain, like the body as a whole, receives its energy from this subtle body, which is to say that the explicate order is powered by the implicate order. There is no "objective" way to measure this, however, since a physical instrument is an explicate order of energy and can measure only things or objects. Scientists have never seen energy of any sort, not even electricity. All that can be seen or measured of any energy form is that energy's physical manifestation, or in this case, the subtle body's effect on the physical.

Consider Kathy and Roy "coming out of the top of their heads." No instruments can detect this kind of action because the subtle energy is more powerful and of a different order than the physical.

Nor could any of us repeat our performance on demand for little men with black boxes. They would have to experience the function themselves, including the long antecedents of passionate quest, gathering of materials, openness to the spirit, or whatever else was needed for them.

Yogic psychology states that perceptions register in the subtle body. The reason research can't determine exactly where perception takes place in the brain is because it *doesn't*. The ghost in the machine is not detectable by the machinery. People in great pain report occasionally that they have left their bodies and looked down at them. When they leave their bodies, body pain no longer has anything to register on.

Yet the subtle body *can* register perceptions independently of the physical body. Ordinarily the two are intricately connected; the subtle permeates the physical and interacts with it point for point; receives its perceptual information; is its twin, powers the body, and yet can detach from it and leave the body on "automatic pilot." When the subtle detaches from the physical, the receptors of the physical senses are no longer in the body, and consciousness is withdrawn from the brain. (Some yogic adepts can withdraw the subtle receptors from specific areas of the body, at which point those parts of the body are anesthetized.)

The fact that our personal awareness can be withdrawn from the body and still retain sensory awareness has a profound significance, of course. And Kathy, Roy, Bob Monroe, and myself are not alone in testifying to this fact. Monroe, for instance, has received well over fifteen thousand letters from readers all over the world. Most have written to tell Bob how relieved they are to learn that their own personal experiences of being out of their body don't indicate craziness after all. How many of us must be hallucinating, psychotic, or plainly lying, if the narrow realism of academics is to be maintained? What an enormous, massive job of doublethink academic science has boxed itself into.

The rather earthshaking fact is that all our abilities we develop in physical life register in, for lack of a term, or are the property of, our subtle body-state. This, then, is the thrust of our biological plan (which will occupy Chapter VI). All ability is organizational, the way for organizing or "assembling" possibility into perceptual experience. Ability, then, is generic, the creative way of establishing order from chaos, and this ability exists in the implicate or subtle order of energy, rather than in the explicate order. The explicate order, our physical world, is the result of our perceptual, organizational ability. Ability is our *most* real, and permanent self. Development of ability is the whole thrust of our biological plan of life, since ability is the vehicle by which we can move *beyond* the physical.

The subtle body is also the vehicle for Shakti, our personal energy of consciousness which powers our brain and body. Our Shakti powers our brain not just as electricity lights a bulb, but also as a broadcasting station fills a television set with its programming. Shakti furnishes both the current to run the set and program which determines the output. Shakti is the energy of the holomovement as expressed within our individual hologram. Our Shakti provides our interaction of brain hologram and the holonomic movement. Shakti projects our world-to-be-in before us. Our brain, body, and senses are parts of this overall projection, the instruments by which we then interact with the physical world projected, and feed our experience back into our subtle body's receptors.

The subtle body, as the recipient of perceptions, is also the seat of emotions, and is a feeling state. Emotions have such power because they are from the subtle, or implicate order. This power can override all sensory information, rational thought, and discrimination. Anxiety is the most powerful and pervasive of all emotions. Since it is a subtle power, anxiety can easily dominate all brain processes, distort all the materials of experience, and sharply interfere with the relation of brain hologram and the holonomic movement, or the mind/brain.

Certain ideas arise out of our anxiety and pass from generation to generation. These ideas form anew in each of us as concepts or brain patterns of organization, right along with our general world view. These concepts then influence the accuracy of the actual holonomic order we *should* perceive and which consciousness powers through us. The actual order powered to us through consciousness is channeled through, and then warped by, the power of concepts formed in anxiety. Since concepts from anxiety arise from the more powerful subtle realm, our surface awareness and thought is shaped by them. We are not consciously aware of these shaping influences, since they are warps in the very power of consciousness giving us our world to view.

Yogic theory calls these warping concepts *samskaras*. A samskara is any impression, feeling, or thought which arises spontaneously in our minds. The brain doesn't generate these randomly, as often assumed; samskaras are the *cause* of random eruptions of thought. Consciousness, the power behind all brain action, moves *from* the causal realm, *through* our subtle body, *into* our physical life, *as* brain action. Samskaras are fixed pre-dispositions carried in our subtle body that warp this otherwise neutral flow of energy and deliver pseudo-information to the brain, which, by its nature, dutifully processes it. The result is a warp in the form consciousness takes in our brain. We can't be aware of this because it constitutes our awareness. Samskaras are part of our subtle body's learned nature, the basis of our outer personality, and not available to our control. Whether of fearful illusion or fond attachment, they disturb the neutral processing of information the brain is designed to provide us, and are always negative in effect. They prevent us from seeing reality as it is, and make true learning, or real change, difficult if not impossible.

Samskaras are the cause of repetitive, automatic (and obstinate) behavior. For instance, I had an in-law once who must have had a resentment samskara. That tendency acted like a form without content. It shaped or influenced her whole life's content according to its resenting-form. Her brain organized and interpreted all of her actual, sensory information according to this samskara of resentment. Everything that took place around her filled her with resentment. She created, of necessity, a continual double-bind for her children, since there was no way they could win her approval or do anything right. She automatically resented everything, including her own resentful nature. Under the impact of this shaping force, her brain would internally create impressions to "feed" this particular tendency, give this form its content. If nothing offered itself immediately to hand, she sat around resenting things that had happened in the past or *might* happen in the future. Since her brain's interpretation of data was "bent" by this powerful subtle-energy warp, her actual perceived reality, the only world available for her, was made *of* that resentful nature. All of which furnished her, of course, with ample ongoing materials for continued resentment, and strengthening of that samskara.

This is one of the ways by which thought becomes "self-generative" as David Bohm spoke of it. The samskara warps the power of consciousness and brings about a repetitive, tape-looped effect in brain processing and resulting perception. The samskara can affect all abilities, interfere with all processes. In the balanced flow of the holonomic movement, we can not know how things really are so long as a samskara is operative.

We inherit samskaras and they influence the way our brain forms its original holographic process. Our sensory apparatus and our resulting sensory world are then shaped by our samskaras and by the ideas they generate. Any sensory experience can fit into the holonomic movement with balance, but only if the receiving-set of brain functions properly. To inherit a samskara is to inherit a disordered brain and to introduce anxiety into the mind/brain.

Fear of something specific doesn't bother our system too much, for then we can organize around meeting that specific fear. Anxiety, though, is fear without a target. Anxiety is a state, a condition of disorder. The disorder is malfunction in our perceptual apparatus caused by samskaras. In childhood, most anxiety generates out of a general fear of abandonment, brought on by failure to bond with the parents. Our later failure to bond with the earth, society, and so on, both confirms and perpetuates that anxiety. All of which means we fail to interrelate with the holonomic movement *even* in its explicate form—that most rudimentary and grossest of energies. Much less are we able to relate with the more powerful and mature realms of development. This final, overall failure to develop the ability to relate we call alienation, or a disorder which acts as an enormous warp on the clarity of the picture consciousness provides.

Autonomy is the goal of development. Autonomy is self-sufficiency, independence, the total freedom of personality. The only real autonomy lies in a self-created and so wholly self-sufficient state. This abstract or mental state lies in the subtle and causal realms, beyond the dissolution of the physical. Autonomy isn't a state so much as the ability to create a state. We are designed to develop such ability through the progressive stages Piaget outlined as our movement from concreteness to abstraction; that is, from early sensory motor experience and learning of the physical world, through to the highest forms of purely mental construction. By the time we reach physical maturity, these abstract abilities needed for autonomy should be roughly functional. Developed or not, however, this drive, which we interpret as personal survival, goes right ahead. This self-preservation proves, perversely enough, the cause of our downfall and ongoing destruction. The very power inherent within our samskaras lies in our drive for autonomy. Once our mind/brain/body organism is warped in its initial unfolding, our system, disordered or not, has no choice but to drive for its autonomy. We have no awareness available except that furnished by our disordered system, and we have no identity other than this awareness. So our very disorder must, of genetic necessity, drive for its own self-sufficiency and independence.

An individual undergoes disordering, it seems, according to his culture's disorder. By the very nature and mechanics of our brain's world-view construction in infancy and childhood, we have no choice but to identify with the construction we make, which we must make. Since we must pattern ourselves and our world-view after our culture and parents, when that is a disordered system for our modeling, we are ourselves disordered in precisely the same way.

To say that our disorder must be reordered, then, is to say that our conceptual structure, which our whole nature must strive to maintain lest we apparently perish, must be essentially de-structured and rebuilt. The initial warp in our developmental drive for wholeness and autonomy must, by the very nature of our brain's drive *for* that development, be interpreted by us as valid, and any move toward actual wholeness or autonomy will be interpreted as a threat to autonomy and resisted at all cost.

The force which alone can straighten us out is the power of insight-intelligence operating through consciousness. And this must, of genetic inevitability, be interpreted by our survival mechanism as antisurvival. Our disorder can't help but drive continually to maintain its own disorder. We strive continually to use the forces of order for maintenance of our own disorder, in spite of ourselves.

This move to use the power of wholeness on behalf of our split-self eternally fails us but eternally pushes us toward maintenance of our error-state. The result is that our whole genetic drive, once warped, can't reorder itself. And change, as yogic theory states, real conceptual change in a human, becomes the rarest single event in the world. Instead of change we get an infinite rationalization, as our drive for autonomy maintains itself.

We can't develop as we must, nor can we make any real change of our personal nature, through any effort of our own. Yet our drive for autonomy must consider any effort other than self-effort as a loss of autonomy. This is the Fall of Man—an eternal process happening anew to each of us, and brought about by our very drive for wholeness which pushes us night and day.

So, samskaras are culturally imposed, impinged upon us through upbringing, schooling, and general traumas. They assure our consensus conformity along cultural lines. We also acquire personal

samskaras which act as fatal flaws, causing repetitive negative re-
actions in us, making us sadly predictable. Our samskaras act like
a "worry organ," the more they are fed, the more insatiable their
appetite.

By the time we are aware of thinking about a particular thing, we
think that we have voluntarily thought such a thing. Perhaps we
have, or perhaps we have simply reacted to a particular samskara
warping the energy of our thought to its use. So there is no moral-
ethical judgment concerning samskaras. They happen to us as fate.
We can't lift ourselves out of this bind by thinking, which is a weak
energy, nor can we stop thinking ordinarily since the nature of the
brain is to think and it is powered from the implicate order to do so.
Because the subtle energy of emotion is directly involved in samskara action, only an energy more powerful even than subtle energy
can break the vicious circle.

In the summer of 1979, I enrolled in the Siddha Yoga courses, six
weeks of study and discipline. We spent some eleven and a half
hours a day cross-legged on the floor, which seemed to push every
samskara button in my being. One day the subject was *Karma,* the
law of action-reaction, cause-effect, or reap as you sow. I recalled a
study sent me of the grossly inhuman treatment of ghetto mothers
in the largest maternity ward in the East, and the damage done the
infants delivered there. I couldn't see how the calloused stupidity of
the medical people involved should be attributed to the Karma of
black babies and so challenged the class, and swami in charge, with
my argument.

The schedule of subjects is tight in the course, and the class
moved on to other realms, rather than dwelling on my obviously
potent point of exception. *My* mind didn't move on, though. My
hostility and bitterness toward the medical profession flared up with
all its old venom; the peculiar emotional potency that ghetto-
mother report originally had on me surged in with renewed vigor.
(Karma my foot! Little infants? Those medicine men should be
hung . . . etc.)

I tried to put the matter out of my mind, but it hung in there, and
grew. My hostility spread to the class, the swami, the course. Siddha
Yoga. Nonsense about Karma, samskaras, and such became re-

volting. My mind reverted back to good old American logic with a vengeance. I was thoroughly tape-looped into this mess when I went to our evening program and sat, not ten feet away, from Muktananda, listening to his talk with only part of my mind.

Suddenly I felt what I can only describe as a white-hot arrow loose from the base of my spine, shoot up to the top of my head, and explode there as a burst of outright anger toward Muktananda himself. No sooner had I reacted to that first burst than it happened again, more intensely: a second whiter-hot arrow shot up, burst in my brain, now no less than rage toward Muktananda, right there in front of me. Since I know all too well that he is quite in touch with his ambient, which includes all those around him, I went into a serious alert. A third "arrow" loosed, almost in slow motion this time, and comprehension began to slowly loose in me as well, though it was to be weeks before I grasped all the implications of this particular lesson.

The experience was a grace, typical of the kind of learning a true spiritual teacher imparts. It was a lesson freely given, a clarification on several levels. First, it gave me a clear demonstration of how samskaras move from some subtle area and arrive in the brain as thoughts, impressions, or emotions, which we then think we have originated but have really only received and reacted to. All that afternoon I had been unable to shake a particular set of hostile thoughts, but was convinced that I was simply being rational. (After all, *I* had read a great deal on child development, birthing practices, and so on. *I* was only being practical and realistic. *These* people and their Sanskrit jargon just didn't grasp what was going on. . . .)

Yet, because of this arrow-experience, I saw, all too clearly, how I had been but a puppet on a string all that afternoon, literally jerked about by impressions over which I had no control, but which brought about an elaborate rationale in me to convince me that I was very much in control, probably the only one around in control, that all was my conscious, intelligent, volitional expertise and "reasoning."

Understand, the issue wasn't the ghetto-birth tragedy, which God knows is tragedy enough. The issue was my hostility toward the world, which remained in me, right below the surface. This general hostility constantly sought its targets. If it failed to find a handy one, it dug one up.

From that moment on, I have been aware that every time an emotion arises on my mental horizon, no matter its content, nature, or "reasonableness," samskaras are at work. I am being acted on, I am not in charge. To say that such a revelation is disarming is an understatement, since it seriously undermines our entire criteria, our whole judgment system. Since our criteria is generally based on anxiety, you can see why my experience was grace, a gift of learning freely given. It was another "block removal"—another step toward freedom from anxiety, though it seemed to rob me of a cornerstone of my thinking.

The lesson also pointed up a fact in my history which I had carefully shielded from awareness. All my adult life, even in my years as an avowed atheist, I had harbored an intense hostility toward God. True to my heritage, though, God had been only a vague abstraction in my life, at best a "principle" or symbol. How can you express hostility toward a vague principle? In my arrow-experience this hidden block was brought out and dispelled through proximity to Muktananda. Which is to say, God had become real and tangible, the general had become specific, the abstraction had become concrete, right before me. So the vague abstraction of hostility could coalesce, materialize, become realized and so dispelled.

Samskaras seem to arise in the same way insight-revelation does, just constantly instead of rarely. Samskaras seem the negative side of the insight function. Actually samskaras, when compared to the power of insight, are a shallow form of subtle energy, but still powerful enough to keep our isolated, self-generative thought spinning around in repetitive tape loops. Thus we repeat ourselves ad nauseam, and, as history shows, we never learn from history.

Bohm speaks of a "deeper level" of thought which springs from insight-intelligence. Disconnected from the holonomic order and propelled by samskaras, however, brain-thinking tries to become (and thinks itself) all levels of thought, and self-sufficient. This breeds a disoriented, semantic world, isolated from intelligence and the balance of the holonomic movement. From such an imbalanced thought-process only disorder and destruction can come, and in this artificial realm, only anxiety is permanent or stable.

The Pueblo chief, Ochwiay Biano, told Carl Jung that white men were ". . . always upset, their faces lined with wrinkles . . . a sign of eternal restlessness." Ochwiay said the whites were crazy since they maintained that they thought with their heads, whereas it was well known that only crazy people did that. Indians, he said, thought with their hearts. (This was some fifty years ago, and Ochwiay was in his eighties.)

Muktananda says the heart is the true seat of the mind. He speaks of the "Primordial Principle in the cave of the heart." I became obsessed with experiencing this true mind, and longed to escape the tyranny of my chattering head. Throughout the fall of 1979 I dwelt continually on somehow opening up this stony organ of mine. I was home for a short stay in November, got up from my early meditation one morning and went over to stoke the fire. I bent to open the stove door and something burst in my chest, slightly to the right of center. Physically it felt as though a bag of hot water had burst under pressure. The burst spread throughout my body as an exquisite warm wave of love, different from any experience I had known. I had to fly West for a university lecture the next day, and the entire trip took place in a state of euphoria, certainty, peace, and clarity.

My heart which had burst open was my "subtle" heart, of course, not old thumper itself, and it is this "implicate order" organ that is the seat of the Self, the abode of God. Here is found the fourth and final body of yogic psychology, the supercausal, the realm of insight-intelligence, the witness state, the final part of us that sees, for whose seeing all the other orders of energy are but instruments. Jung and Krishna Prem both referred to this Self as "that mysterious circle whose center is everywhere and circumference nowhere."

Development, from conception to maturity, is genetically designed to move from the explicate order into this Self, in neat, logical stages. A fully developed mind can move through many states for witnessing, without being lost, or "trapped" in any of them: the brain and its physical and psychological interaction with the world; day-dreams, night-dreams, and autonomously created states as found in hypnagogic imagery, shared hypnotic states, lucid dreaming, and so on; a theoretical state of pure creative energy from which anything can be made; and, just the awareness of our witness state itself, untrammeled and free.

In religious ecstasy, as in the play insight I described earlier, we are probably in the subtle body, the source of feeling and emotion. There we take our impressions not from the world, but directly from insight-intelligence. That is why these experiences, while powerful and numinous, can be reported.

An "introverted mystical experience," however (to use Walter Stace's term), goes beyond all sensory perception, beyond ecstasy or emotion, and so beyond the subtle body. This is the "peace which passeth all understanding." No verbal description can be made of this state, since "understanding" is, indeed, left behind. (Often we can clearly detect our passing through the subtle state as we go into the causal and supercausal realms.)

Finally, an "extroverted mystical experience" occurs when ordinary, brain-oriented, physical life, with its sensory input from the explicate order, suddenly unifies with the holonomic movement itself. Here all creation becomes a unity both fluid and perfect, a pristine and infinite whole, where, indeed, we see the world in a grain of sand. This happy state seems to be a perfect balance between all the four bodies, truly Self-awareness. This is reportedly the normal functional state of a Siddha master, a "realized being." What he has realized is that he *is* the holonomic order, that he is consciousness and that everything is consciousness.

The light of this consciousness, from all reports, seems to be an electric-blue color. Probably the most common occurrence we have around Muktananda is seeing this color in various ways. Generally this energy appears as a tiny seed of light, what is called the *bindu,* or "blue pearl." Variations of it occur continually. Tiny blue points of brilliance and beauty, they often leap out from Baba's person in the darkened meditation hall. Occasionally they spring from my pages of manuscript here in my typewriter, when work goes well. On three occasions, as I worked Rudrani Farbman's Shaktipat story into Chapter VII (Form and Content), that page turned into a blaze of blue which persisted no matter how I looked away. I had to concentrate and look through the brilliance to see the text I was retyping. (*Suggestion,* the psychologist scoffs; to which I reply: Indeed, and give me more! More! The power of the Word is profound beyond our comprehension.)

David, from Los Angeles, lived in the Oakland ashram when Baba was there in 1976. At five every morning, David walked from the "annex" to the ashram proper, some four blocks through a reportedly dangerous neighborhood. On one particular morning it was pitch-black out, but instead of being apprehensive, David sensed a peacefulness from everywhere. Suddenly, right in front of him appeared the "blue pearl," a tiny intense point of brilliant blue from which radiated every conceivable color. The light remained at the same distance in front of him throughout his walk, a source of "majesty, beauty, and eternal constancy." Then the pearl "went behind my sense of sight, its presence still there, its essence with me as a barometer of my spiritual practice, a criterion of my relations with the world and my inner Self."

Marsha Mason, the actress, reports the following from an intensive in Miami Beach in December 1979: "The lights were still dim when I caught a glimpse of Baba coming into the hall. . . . Suddenly I realized there was this funny blue stuff all around his outline . . . I blinked my eyes and said 'What is that? Where is that blue stuff coming from?' I didn't want to believe what I was seeing. . . . He [didn't] have his glasses on . . . his head swung in my direction; I looked into his eyes and there were these beautiful dancing blue lights. 'Well,' I said, 'I don't believe this. My mind is playing tricks on me . . . the light is coming from somewhere . . . a reflection or something.'. . . As I sat there the blue light just kept dancing around, shimmering, and I began to just enjoy it and accept it. . . . Baba turned his face again toward where I was sitting and I felt this quick instant flash going from him to me and it landed right here in my forehead. I reached up to touch my forehead and it was burning hot. 'I didn't expect all of this,' I said. 'It's really burning. Even my hands can tell it's burning . . . this is no trick.' So I shut my eyes and right there I saw Nityananda's form all in blue and Baba standing right behind him, all in blue. So . . . I realized that I had this spiritual experience because . . . I let enough room for Baba to come in."

Rénée Weber, writing about Bohm's new paradigm for physics, laments that: " . . . even those in full intellectual accord with this view encounter difficulty coming to grips with it on the existential level of their lives." Which translates as: Bohm's theory touches on our true longing but we can't seem to grab hold of it.

Only meditation can bridge the gap, Bohm says, at which point I fear he may lose even those in "intellectual accord" with his theory. The problem with "coming to grips with [it] on the existential level of our lives" is that this observation is backward—upside down. The existential must be *gripped* by that holonomic order, something the academic mind cannot tolerate. Marsha had only to "let enough room for Baba to come in." Which is to say, when her thought stepped aside she could move into a far wider spectrum of reality. We have been conditioned to believe that that which *can't* be gripped by our ordinary thought is hallucination or illusion. We have been conditioned to believe that any incursion of the really great creative energies is pathological. So, for the culturally fragmented person, any move toward wholeness is interpreted as a threat, a final fragmentation or loss of coherence. When the instrument of body/brain becomes self-generative, anything not available to its weak energy must be interpreted as destructive. Thus our perceptions become inverted, we see things backward, and turn heaven into hell.

We have only to *let,* to allow, and stop gripping. Not because of some divine decree or moral imperative, but simply because of the mechanics of energy, and the nature of our mind and brain.

V

Keys and Locks

"Man is born like a Garden ready Planted & Sown. This world is too poor to produce one Seed." So proclaimed the visionary poet, William Blake, nearly two centuries ago.

Since our mind/brain has enfolded within it the holonomic movement as well as our individuality, Blake's metaphor proves apt. As any gardener knows, though, a host of misadventures lie in wait for every garden. Many a weed can grow, the original planting hindered or lost should cultivation be faulty. A perfect plant may be locked into a seed, but it must await the proper keys of nourishment to unlock it. Since a perfect development is possible only through alignment with the holonomic order, the key to that alignment is the pearl of great price—to mix all the metaphors.

An infant has an open-ended intelligence locked into his genes, but the key for unlocking lies with parent and society. Only intelligence can breed, stimulate, and foster intelligence. The medium for that fostering is culture.[1] Culture is an artificial, man-made ambient for growing people; and every culture specializes in the kind of person it grows. Every culture fosters some particular potential at the expense of some other, defining itself by its own, arbitrary definitions.

Cross-cultural studies show how cultures will shut out and ignore, or stimulate and foster, different capacities. For an estimated
thirty thousand years (the date gets pushed back continually) the
Australian Aborigine maintained a culture based on a particular
mental set called Dream-Time. Dream-Time was a state of consciousness which encompassed the whole aboriginal world. In that
state the Aborigine had available to him whatever he needed from
his environment: when in Dream-Time he could tell where his
kinsmen were, where his "totem animals" were (those he was allowed to eat), where the water was, what the weather was like over a
wide terrain, and so on. In addition, Dream-Time was a state of euphoria.

An English group studying the Aborigine had one of their group
travel a course of some one hundred miles, covering a varied terrain
of swamp, shifting sand, rock, forest, and so on, carefully marked
on a map. One year later, when any possibility of a sign remaining
seemed remote, they asked an Aborigine tracker if he could follow
the course. He replied yes, if they would give him an article of
clothing worn by the man leaving the trail. Holding the item, the
Aborigine went into Dream-Time. There he "got in touch with the
Two Great Brothers who eternally, instant by instant, create the
universe." In touch with this genesis, he was automatically in touch
with the man whose article he held, and the event of laying down
the trail. The Aborigine then broke into his loose, economical run,
and followed the trail unerringly, without stopping to look for
traces, if any could have conceivably remained.

Within Bohm's holomovement, or Siddha theory, the event is
perfectly reasonable. The event of a year before was "enfolded"
within the present moment. To unfold that event, the Aborigine
needed only some item related to that time as a key to unlock that
enfoldment. The elaborate intellectual organization of Aborigine
society (Lévi-Strauss called it one of the most rigorously intellectual
systems in history) gravitated around the individual's ability to
enter into consciousness and remain in a perfect balance with his
world.

Yet the Aborigine never built even the rudest shelter nor would
he wear clothes. Except for his spear and boomerang, he rigorously

eschewed all tools and technologies. (Lest we think him too stupid, however, consider the boomerang: one of the most sophisticated applications of a flying wing ever conceived. When thrown by the mature Aborigine, the boomerang could travel three hundred yards without varying from about eighteen inches aboveground, just the height to bring down an animal. If the boomerang failed to hit its target, it followed its smooth ellipse to land, spent, at its thrower's feet—sheer genius in the economy of motion.)

We looked askance at the Aborigine's animal-like existence—a creature too dumb to build a house or wear clothes. Yet we developed technology by, and live under, an equally rigid emphasis on certain other processes of thought. As it turns out, the Aborigine so rigorously screened out possessions and "progress" *in favor of* his Dream-Time with its perfect ecological rapport. Under the impact of the white man, most Aborigine adopted clothes and a house—or were forced into them—and his Dream-Time collapsed, leaving him a derelict, lost to his own history. (I understand that a remnant of the people still maintain the "totem," and I can only hope it will somehow be preserved.)

Back in the 1950's several studies were made of fire-walking[2] in Ceylon and other countries, where this phenomenon plays a striking role in religious observance. To walk barefoot, back and forth, across a twenty-foot bed of coals that will melt aluminum on contact is, to say the least, not in our culture's set of expectancies or acceptances. We dismiss such activity as "autosuggestion," whatever in the world that could mean, in order to maintain a belief system which excludes any act of personal power as possible.

A capacity can be lost to a culture, or never developed at all. Consider how we have lost a natural bonding to our infants at birth. Such a capacity can be regained, or rediscovered and developed, only through outside intervention, or by some fluke of thought outside our developed world-view. Even then, maintenance of our culture's and its professions' definitions of itself can create a closed circuit blocking such intervention and enlightenment.

Many potentials are missed through failure of response from parents, who were in turn not developed in those potentials by their parents, and so on in infinite regress. Every capacity conceivable to imagination is inborn in us, since ours is an open-ended mind/brain, but any specific capacity must be brought forth and developed.

For instance, language is genetic but develops only if language is used around the infant/child, and, of course, develops according to the kind of language used. The newborn infant begins apparently random physical movements almost immediately. But locked into those movements is a precise "repertoire" of muscular responses to the parts of speech. The moment speech is used around the infant those otherwise random movements immediately coordinate with the sounds. Each part of speech elicits an invariable and precise physical movement. Physical movement coordinating with speech sound is the way that the new brain "learns" language, or creates its structure of language. (And this has been recorded from two minutes after birth in scores of infants.) Actual speech is the key that unlocks the potential for speech in the infant/child, and virtually all learning is through this kind of modeling—since an "interweaving of energies" is involved, a patterning.

There is a threefold law of development: a desired function must be modeled or presented by an adult or superior to stimulate, or synchronize with, an initial response in the child. The child is triggered genetically to "interweave energies" and construct his model of the world, but he must be given a model for that construction. Then the child must be given an ongoing model to follow throughout this development. Single exposures can seldom be "mathematically interrelated" by the new holonomic expression. Finally, the ability involved must be allowed to unfold in its natural stages, according to nature's timetable and overall plan. The key must unlock the door at the appropriate time and have the patience to keep it open.

Language is genetic to us because it is one of the tools intelligence uses for development of thought. Sound is a vibratory energy, as is matter and the thing-events of this world. The earliest preparation for speech is sensory-motor, or sound-muscle activity (all early learning is sensory-motor), and the names we give our young for the thing-events of their life, and their "knowledge" of those thing-events, are built into that young brain as a unified, single pattern of energy-vibration. Word and the thing it names are a single impulse in the brain, and our primary world-view is based on this unity of word-event.

Naming is not just an arbitrary convenience we adopt for communication. Indeed, communication may be an almost incidental by-product of naming. Nor are words inadequate and misleading substitutes for the "real thing." As Northrop Frye expressed it: "An object that has received a name is more real by virtue of it than an object without one. A thing's name is its numen, its imaginative reality in the eternal world of the human mind. . . . Reality is intelligibility, and a poet who has put things into words has lifted 'things' from the barren chaos of nature into the created order of thought."

The early child goes through a period of passionate intensity for naming everything he sees (the "Whazzat Mamma?" period). This is verbal-modeling, and the word given is the key that unlocks that particular part of the "barren chaos of nature" and grows an orderly arrangement within that brain—that is, forms a concept. The capacity of the word to lift things from the undifferentiated event into perceptual order is precisely what the child's brain needs to organize its world-view and give, in turn, a world for the child to view. In this way the movement from concreteness to abstraction is begun. The created order of thought will eventually be the eternal world of the human mind—the final matrix into which we must move when physical life is over.

The two-year-old will move his hand when asked to say the word *hand* because the word and thing are as one in his brain, and because language builds into the brain through sound-muscle response. This response continues throughout the early years. Five-year-old Fred can't conceive of himself being named other than what he was named, since his name is not an appendage or something after the fact. His name doesn't stand for his person. His name is his numen, too, that which lifts his perceptual awareness of his own identity into order.

All brain function grows from the original unity of mind/brain/world, and moves toward an increasing flexibility and creative possibility. But the unity of word and thing is a permanent part of brain function, and maintains the stability of our adult world-view. This original unity is the "picture" which consciousness powers into our brain and which is projected out as our world. Out of this stability, language should grow into an art of its own, an abstract creative system. (The limitations inherent within language do not lie with the nature of language, but with the strength of the intelligence using it.)

Originally the word is the key which unlocks the thing-event from chaos, and the brain builds key and lock in as a single entrainment. A word grows in its power and scope with the development of a verbal thinking, or logic, which can finally separate key from lock, separate the word from its thing. The child's concrete thinking automatically moves his hand when saying the word hand at age two, but development should burst all such concrete boundaries. Like intelligent thought, a word need never stand still. The word should become " . . . a storm center of meanings, sound, and associations, radiating out indefinitely like the ripples of a pool . . ." to use Frye's description of a word's possibility in the hands of a poet.

By its very nature of being our system of definition, as well as our particular vehicle for words, culture limits potential even as culture is the formal means for unlocking potential. Culture is a language-made affair, an artifice of words and verbal concepts, a man-made function we automatically sustain and which then enters into shaping us as we are. Enculturation is a part of that single-entrainment word-thing unity of brain, and the conceptual pattern that remains the permanent basis of all future thought and perception. So long as a culture is based on isolated thought, and has become self-generative, it acts not as a key unlocking potential, but as a lock preventing anything not within its system of prediction and control.

Our semantic passion for precise word meaning may arise from this desire for prediction and control. We wish to control another's reception of meaning from our own speech, and look for a kind of one-for-one correspondence we can count on. Eastern thought seems to treat a word more as a "storm center of meaning and associations." The Hindu, for instance, seems to coin a new word for God with each breath, and will use the same word in a confusing variety of ways. This allows flexibility of thought, but it can easily lead to fuzzy, imprecise, and evasive thinking. Much obscurity can hide behind such a practice. Verbal thinking of this sort can be effective analogically, but cloak laziness of mind. Words like *fate* and *Karma* can become refuges to avoid the risk and difficulty of clear analytical thought.

Western thought, on the other hand, tends to define for a precision which finally allows little flexibility and gets isolated in its own definition, cut off from relationship with a living, moving reality. The definition will tend to exist for its own formal sake, become self-generative and sterile, cut off from the real blood-pulse of life. Our part-thinking can also cloak laziness of mind, create screens by which we try to evade such large-scale effects as *Karma* and *fate*. We think our closed-in definitions give us prediction and control, put our lives more squarely in our own hands; and we are continually upset that our controls continually fail us, that we can't get ourselves in hand.

Surely a balance of our polar modes of thought would unlock our potential and lead to a creative culture. But the balance can't come from either mode of thought. Only the power of the bond brings balance.

No capacity can unfold without an appropriate model and proper nurturing, however, just as *any* capacity will unfold if given a model and nurturing at the appropriate time. A child could imitate, or construct a model of his universe, around any model, and respond according to his construction. He *does* model what he is given, and so does as we do. He is blocked not because of some innate lack, but from an outer lack of models and nurturing.

This is why Shaktipat and its resulting personal power are virtually unknown in the West (and rare enough anywhere). An appropriate stimulus and nurturing can be given only by a person who has developed such a capacity of balanced, disciplined openness. We do not model our lives according to theories or abstract functions, but according to live, visible, tangible models. We do not bond to universal processes but to persons. The power of the bond can come into our life only through the power of the bonded person.

How, then, can a parent model for and stimulate personal power in a child unless that parent has such power to begin with? A double bind is inherent here, truly a case of don't go near the water until you can swim. This double bind can be broken, and the power of the bond established, however, by that parent finding a personal model of wholeness and at least *practicing* a discipline of wholeness. For the child will immediately model the parent's own model. (All of us did just this in our enculturation.) Fortunately a total, final "enlightenment" is not necessary, or the vicious circle could never be broken.

So, if the West seems spiritually dead, with personal power vanishing if not gone, our models of spirit and power are weak or missing, even as our scientific-technological models are all too prevalent and powerful. By their fruits you can know them. If our keys are not unlocking a quality of life in harmony and creation, we should switch keys.

Science should be a key unlocking phenomena, instead of a lock shutting out any phenomena not fitting its keys of preconception. The original claim of science to be dispassionate analysis of evidence could lead to a wonderful understanding and creativity, were it bonded to the actual holonomic movement instead of being limited to the explicate order. That is, were it not limited to such an extremely weak and narrow segment of "evidence" acceptable *for* analysis. The only way the broad spectrum of evidence available could be accepted would be for the mind/brain to be reinstated as a criteria, rather than weak, explicate-order machines and instruments.

Our idea system must be flexible enough to incorporate anything occurring in our lives, not a system ruling out large areas of possibility as hallucination and illusion. A viewpoint which relates only to the explicate order and its "objective experience" automatically establishes a serious tyranny over the mind. Through such definitions we allow only the "merest ripple" on the surface of the holonomic movement into our lives.

A great richness is shut out when we deny ourselves access to the implicate and insight realms of our own mental process. Consider, for instance, how a psychologist would view David's history (that same David from Los Angeles mentioned before). David was twenty-four when he met Muktananda, and felt that he "immediately understood Baba's explanation of the Self within." While working at his job, David began to hear singing in his head. It sounded like pure music that was expressed as words, a single phrase that carried all meaning. It was "the play of consciousness in all things." For some three years this singing continued, explaining the mundane world in terms of the absolute, deconditioning all David's culturally induced anxieties, bringing him into harmony with his outer world and giving peace within.

David's inner work of healing and development came through avenues unique to David. Siddha Yoga considers this inner guidance a form of Shakti, the universal energy. Shakti is both universal and personal. Yogic theory considers Shakti feminine, active, and creative. She is also the bond of power, holding the holonomic movement in its unity. She sometimes bears a striking resemblance to Carl Jung's *anima* figure. At any rate, David's Shakti didn't check the current textbooks to make sure her approach was objective and academically acceptable. David was the subject and the subjective approach was what was needed. A disordered brain can't be ordered through objective experience. How could perception of outside objects straighten out one's internal perceptual apparatus? If a TV set is faulty, no amount of great programming by some station is going to correct that set.

Obviously, had David publicly acclaimed the fact of this singing in his head he might well have been hospitalized, given shock treatments, blasted with drugs, and so on, to straighten him out. And obviously we couldn't duplicate David's Shakti performance under laboratory conditions to test its "realness." What explicate-order instrument could register what Shakti, our subtle power, is doing? What weak-energy system can handle this bonding-power?

Nor could David himself repeat the performance. Shakti never repeats herself. Each of her moves is creation itself. She creates her paths as she moves. "Behold, I make all things new," the Gospel proclaimed. Keys of preconception can't fit this lock of potential. The preconceived can only duplicate its own dull rounds. (How incredibly, unbelievably, intolerably *dull* modern psychology is. This dullness, more than its stupidity, is its final offense.) Dull rounds can be duplicated, even predicted and controlled. Shakti can't. Shakti is both the bonding-power and the potential yet to be bonded into experience; she is both key and lock.

We are always creating our culture even as we are being molded by our creation. Our isolated, self-generative creations are always out of balance and essentially destructive, over time. They lock us in and every movement for freedom tightens the lock. Only through the bond, through holonomic alignment, could culture be the key unlocking our potential. Culture and potential should stand as key and lock; they should relate like form and content as with any creative work. As culture is our own creation, it is the key to our creativity, and so should be our greatest work of art.

VI

The Biological Plan

Developmentalists all seem to agree that brain development and learning is a movement from the concrete to the abstract.[1] We can also say that it is movement from the physical toward the mental; or from an identity with matter to identity with mind; or from consciousness to thought; or from implicate to explicate orders of energy. The goal of development is autonomy, or self-sufficiency, of the personality which emerges out of this movement. Autonomy can only be achieved by moving, at some point, beyond the mechanics of concreteness, including the brain, from which the whole expression manifests.

Nature has designed us so that our development from concreteness to abstraction takes place through a series of shifts from one *matrix* to another. *Matrix* is the Latin word for womb. The word designates a threefold condition: a source of possibility; energy to explore that possibility; and a safe place for that exploration to unfold. The womb of the mother is, fittingly enough, the ideal example: it provides a source of possibility for new life; energy for that possibility to be explored by that new life; and a safe environment for that exploration.

To shift from the womb, or from any matrix, is to be "born out of it" and into another one. The nature of our growth is such that each matrix is larger than and less constricting, or more abstract and less concrete than the previous one. Each matrix encompasses more possibility and power, and should provide an increasingly safer place to stand.

At each matrix-shift, the brain undergoes a growth-spurt which prepares it for massive and rapid new learning. The mind/brain learns by exploring the new matrix and constructing a conceptual pattern of it—which means a sensory integration of that matrix; a structure of knowledge of it, as Piaget would say; or a "mathematical interweaving of energies" between the explicate and implicate orders, as Bohm might say.

The mind/brain unfolds new mental capacities at each growth-spurt and, in turn, needs corresponding new physical capacities suitable to the kind of matrix-exploration designed to take place. Biological growth provides just this new physical capacity since the body is an instrument of the brain and develops in conjunction with the brain's needs at each stage.

Consider the triune nature of our brain which brain research finds in its dissections: the reptilian brain is the hind-brain, the old mammalian brain is the mid-brain, the new brain is the cerebral cortex with its various lobes and hemispheres. This triune nature fits child development in the first seven years, too, or, as I need to emphasize over and again, what child development is *meant* to be.

Each need of the new holographic brain clearly unfolds for its fulfilling, and the body, its instrument, clearly develops in precise synchrony to meet those needs. Infant helplessness, for instance, is designed so that the new holographic brain system might make its initial construction, its first impressions, from and of a human standpoint. The mother's body, particularly her face, is the matrix after birth, the focus of infant attention.

Following this period of human orientation, the oldest brain system, the reptilian brain, takes over with its demand for, its intent-toward, creeping and crawling. The body dutifully responds with appropriate new physical processes as the old brain impells movements of interaction that give a snake's eye view of the world. Sensory integration of brain and world, a structure of knowledge or interweaving of energies in the new hologram, begins from this most basic viewpoint. A new universe will form from the point of immediate sensory contact. This simplest and grossest interweaving of energy gives the grounds for ever more complex, subtle, and far-ranging ones.

When this primary base is functional, the period of the old mammalian brain takes over: new physical abilities spring forth, walking begins, a passion for climbing—anything to gain the new, upright perspective and its vastly wider interaction and interweaving of the explicate order of things.

For seven years (more or less) this world-construction takes place in that new holographic system; the impetus for movement and exploration comes from the older brain systems and the resulting interactions register (for lack of a term) as conceptual patterns in the new brain. This leads to volition and eventual creativity. By age four, some 80 percent of this explicate construction is complete. During this time the parent is the matrix, the point of departure.

Around age four the first *subtle* energies begin to manifest. This manifestation must await certain divisions of labor in the brain, to be discussed shortly. These subtle energies will furnish the bonds to the new matrix into which the child is designed to move around age seven.

At age seven (or thereabout) several great occurrences take place. The brain undergoes a growth spurt which prepares for new learning and the development of subtle power. Now that the world-construction is made, that world becomes the matrix, the new source of possibility, new energy to explore that possibility, and the safe place to make that exploration. We can say that mind has produced a brain, which has produced a body to move with, and a world to move in.

At seven a complete logical shift happens virtually overnight, according to Piaget. This logical shift changes the entire operation, interweaving of energies, or processing of information, within that mind/brain. Now that the bulk of the explicate order has been created anew in that new hologram, the new personality begins a foray into his own creation. He begins to explore how his personal power can interact with his newly formed world out there. Which is to say he begins to explore the *subtle* area of self, a more abstract manifestation, while standing in the concreteness of his created world.

Piaget saw this through academic eyes as "concrete operational thinking"—which is mind's ability to operate on information coming into the brain and to change that information according to logic, or an idea. In *Magical Child*, I explored a more realistic aspect of this interaction: since the world-view is also the world *viewed*, a change of information concerning that world can change that world itself—within certain limits. And this is what the exploration of subtle body and physical body, in their dynamic interaction, or "concrete operation," is all about.

Our subtle body, or state, is the seat of our personal power. Personal power is conceptual ability, the capacity to interweave and interrelate energy frequencies creatively, put them into meaningful order. All of our capacity is subtle energy, since capacity means the power to organize.

The child from age seven to about eleven is designed genetically to explore the new matrix in the making. That new matrix is the *combination* of earth and personality's capacity for organization, or creation. Capacity, a subtle energy, is potentially a greater power than that weaker explicate order which the brain has just finished constructing. So the explicate order is subject to the person's ability, at least theoretically. The young person, somewhere after seven, begins a foray into using his subtle, personal powers of organization and creation for altering, changing, playing with, the concrete world he has made. This is a first-level abstraction, or "concrete operational thinking." The child is limited only by and to his models for imitation and the possibilities opened to him and suggested to him, during this period. The key and lock factor holds. If he is given nothing more than paper and scissors, paste and paints, he does accordingly.

At age eleven another brain growth-spurt and logical shift takes place, new physical apparatus unfolds, and "formal operational thinking" begins. This is the ability of the mind to operate on and change the very conceptual structure of the brain, in addition to being able to operate on information coming into that brain. As a result processes can be separated from the original concreteness (the given explicate order) entirely, and the period of true abstract thinking begins. This means the ability to either receive or (eventually) create information or ideas not generated by the physical world at all, and, in fact, having no relation with it.

The push now is for more than just altering, changing, or making things out of the physical world. Now the push is for a second-level abstraction: making things out of pure imagination. The seeds of that imagination will still spring from the earth and interactions with it as gained from age seven to eleven. But the mind/brain will work for the ability to create a reality not directly dependent on any aspect of the explicate order.

This new matrix-construction that takes place (or should) after age eleven is a preliminary move into the "causal body," into the realm of a "vast energy beyond the implicate order," as Bohm expressed it. The implicate order has the explicate order *implied* within it, but consciousness without such implications offers a pure, original creativity.

This period of exploring abstract creation follows roughly the same four-year cycle found in the concrete operational stage. Formal operation, in turn, is followed, around age fifteen or so, with the same pattern of brain growth-spurt, logical shift, new physical processes (including genital sexuality), and exploration of Reversibility Thinking.

Piaget calls Reversibility Thinking the rarest of all human faculties. Again he saw the function as it rarely occurs in academic settings. And again I would point to its far wider application in the totality of mind/brain. Reversibility Thinking is the initial foray into the final development of human ability. This is the movement into the *supercausal* realm, the state of the fourth "body," insight-intelligence itself.

Reversibility Thinking traces thought back to its source. This is the equivalent of getting your Pawn into the opposite King's row, where that Pawn then becomes Queen. Then she can move anywhere, in any direction. And that is the fourth state of development: the mind/brain can move anywhere, in any direction, within the holonomic order: into the physical world; the subtle dimensions or "astral worlds"; into pure creativity without precedents; or just the silent-witness state, that "peace which passeth all understanding."

Reversibility Thinking is the equivalent of achieving an insight-revelation, a creative Eureka! experience, and being able to turn around and trace that process backward to its source, and repeat it ad lib; which is to say, the ability to perceive and create on any and all possible levels, knowing what you are doing. Thus the human *should* mature: the child should become the father; the man should become God.

Were childhood successful it would lead to a full and rich mature life. The *Guru Gita* (song of the Guru or Holy Spirit) states that the four goals of life are: righteousness, wealth, pleasure, and liberation: a pretty hard menu to beat. When childhood is a developmental bust, adult life is our "norm" of anxiety and alcohol. Were physical life successful, as genetically planned, it would lead to a full and rich "astral" or subtle body existence. When physical life is a bust (our norm), the subtle that follows cannot conceivably be any better. As the child is father to the man, life is father to life after death.

Very few humans develop in adult life because their child development was too inadequate to provide adequate *tools* of development. Very few humans develop sufficient mental tools in physical life to enter into the subtle realm successfully at death. So the subtle realm ends in a cosmic dumping-ground, a confused mess mirroring the physical mess. How could it be any different?

The nature of our mind/brain is to build an infinitely flexible system of accommodation and adaptation to new information and to create new information itself. The formula is: construct a knowledge of the Earth as it is (recreate the holonomic order anew in a new holographic brain creation); construct a system for extracting information, ideas, and abilities out of that tangible Earth-knowledge; and then construct a system for creating new information and new abilities out of those extractions. This movement can also be represented as the implicate order giving birth to the explicate order, which matures into an implicate expression able to create out of its own infinite potential.

Psychologists speak of the child as egocentric. The child sees himself as the center of the universe; the world moves out from him as an extension of his own being. This egocentric view is not an error of child-logic but the truth, the way the hologram of the brain forms in the early years. For the new brain to make its construction of knowledge is equally to project that knowledge out as the world.

The child considers his body an extension of his self and the world as an extension of his body because that is the truth within the holonomic order of things.

The child can't see the world as something other than his own being until his holographic brain constructs a process for separating his sense of I-ness, his sense of being, from a that-ness or other-ness, out beyond him. A child's emerging sense of I-ness can't help but identify with his simultaneous construction of his world and the names given him in that construction work, including his self as his own given name. A representative of the holonomic system, which every brain starts out to be, can't be other than a single unit.

This single-unit brain must then, after completion of its world, construct a "division of labor" within its construction, a means to separate the holonomic patterns of unity, on the one hand, from a pattern of unique awareness, or individuality, on the other. A secondary system must be set up within the otherwise single functioning brain system, before name can begin to detach from the thing-named, self from world, individual from his continuum, or thought from consciousness. This secondary system is called *individuation.* Individuation is, in effect, an abstraction out of the holonomic unity, the primary process, of the brain system.

This birth of the individual out of the holonomic order requires a logical shift in brain-processing as well as brain mechanisms for that shift. This mechanism and shift will divide the brain's work load between world-view maintenance (the explicate order) and a fluid, personal power and individual viewpoint that (should) draw on the implicate order. That is, what should result is thought resting in the power of consciousness, open to insight.

A huge network of nerve fibers called the *corpus callosum,* connecting the two hemispheres of the brain, begins its growth somewhere in the second year of life, and is completed somewhere in the fourth year. This is the last brain apparatus to form, other than the periodic growth-spurts involved in new learning cycles.

Nature delays this connecting link's completion until the child's brain has roughed in its basic world-construction. (Remember that this primary world is a single holonomic gestalt with I at the center; where child and world, like word and object, are identical.) Only when the basic world-view has been roughed in is the job of separating an individual awareness out of that holonomic unity either possible or suitable to nature's plan—just as it takes nine months for development of the uterine infant before a division of infant and uterus is suitable. Individuation, which begins around age four, can be considered, in fact, as simply an extension of birth, the slow separation of personality from creative process. So the resulting egocentricity is not an error of child-logic, but the simple mechanism of brain—the way each of us is born into this world is the way a world is born for us to be in.

Specializations, such as building a logical thought independent of the concreteness of word and thing, or an individual awareness separate from its egocentric and holonomic order, can't begin until these connecting links between the hemispheres are functional. By that time (around age four) the child's world-view is largely functional and evenly distributed in the brain as its fundamental world-pattern. This basis will never be violated. Individuality, and all logical, abstract refinements will be extractions out of this basic brain pattern, extractions which can't disturb that stable world. In this way, the world becomes the new matrix, the materials from which an ongoing and creative reality can grow.

This division of labor begins (or becomes noticeable) around the fourth year and reaches its first functional stage around seven. At age seven, that brain growth-spurt and logical shift mentioned above prepare for the massive new learnings which exploration of the physical world as a personal power entails. This relating is an abstraction out of concreteness, through that division of labor in the brain, an abstraction that leaves the original holonomic unity intact.

Five-year-old Fred can't conceptually grasp that he could have been named Jim, since identity and name unfold as a single concept. This identity with name is the same as his identity with his world. That he is *not* the center of his universe, with all an extension of his being, grows in awareness roughly as word and thing-named separate through the division of labor in the brain. As child and mother begin separation at four, to allow for the child's bonding with the Earth and exploration of that new matrix-relationship, so person and Earth begin a slow separation at seven. This separation will prepare for bonding with the next matrix, the world of creative thought, the causal realm. But still all this is only a functional separation within the holographic brain process, a function which leaves intact the actual unity of the holonomic movement enfolded there. Which is to say, that all separation is an abstraction out of, and in a way a kind of illusion, made for the sake of creativity. But underlying any abstraction of separation is a unity which can't be broken, and is the "ultimate reality" behind all creative play, or appearances.

Relationship is the key. Within the implicate order everything is "enfolded" but nothing unfolded—anything is possible but nothing realized. The infant in the womb has a symbiotic relationship with the mother's body, but this is a limited relationship. Only through separation from this matrix can a larger matrix be explored. The second matrix, mother as person, gives a much greater area of exploration, and a richer relationship than the symbiotic one. From the mother, the child radiates out, and nature provides the new physical tools as needed, to explore and construct a knowledge of the world. When this world-knowledge is roughed in, the child begins his separation from the mother, around age four, in order to shift to the world as matrix. His possibilities for relating to his mother are then far larger again, and his possibilities for relating with the world will involve the same kind of functional separation for the same reason—a more flexible relationship, as well as movement into a more rarified, less constricting matrix. Finally, the whole of our explicate-order experience, our physical life, can be seen as a separating from the implicate and insight realms in order to relate to them on a new creative basis.

So we can see that only by a separation from the holomovement, or from God, can we know and relate to God—which is to say, can God know or relate to his own Self. The concrete actuality always is our absolute unity with God, though this can be known only developmentally. Only through maturity can true relationship unfold. This means that genetic development is the key in every respect. The biological plan is in every way a "divine plan."

Nature provides that each division, separation, and addition in child development takes place in proper sequence. If nature is violated, overall maturation must fail. For instance, should the child be separated from egocentricity too soon by enforced premature autonomy or a premature academic schooling, maturation will falter and that child will remain largely in a sensory-motor stage of development (where the bulk of our populace remains). Should the unity of word and thing-named be artificially broken up (rather than developed through maturation), as happens through premature literacy, maturation will again falter. (We might achieve some semantic brilliance in a self-enclosed, self-verifying semantic world, but maturation will be thwarted and anxiety result.) The body is an instrument of the brain. If the brain's unity of word and thing is broken up too soon, before the brain's system of separation is ready, egocentricity is shattered before separation is appropriate or functional. Then not only is there isolation and alienation of personality instead of individuation, but specific bodily disruptions can occur as well. If individuation ends in isolation, instead of autonomy there is anxiety; instead of creativity a clinging to matter as matrix; a fear of change and inability for creative, abstract thought.

When this happens, relationship with the holonomic order is blocked, can't develop, and personality locks into thought as an isolated, self-generative system; then identification remains rooted in the body, no relationship to the larger body of the Earth takes place, and maturation breaks down. Egocentricity is shattered and ego, or I-ness doesn't develop into creative dominion over its world, but remains a homeless waif. Egocentricity, a passing developmental stage, warps into a permanent condition of ego-eccentricity, an isolated I-ness off-center and out of balance with its own holonomic order of mind/brain.

Somewhere in early adolescence, individuation should be complete, and abstract (or formal operational) thought should become functional. This means that personality should begin to relate to and identify with consciousness and insight-intelligence on a functional basis. Personality should become an instrument of that creative thrust, the holonomic structure. For personality is the unique individual form of the holonomic order, its recreation of itself. Personality is the ultimate creation, the sum total of awareness.

Mature life should be an ongoing process of personality's bonding to the next, nonphysical matrix, and the source of that bonding should be the creative power for living fully on this Earth. Traditional cultures celebrated this critical juncture with "rites of passage"—initiation out of childhood into adulthood. Perhaps this ushered in a formal, functional relationship with the whole order of things—and may have been an awakening of one's personal Shakti.

Obviously our developmental process breaks down. Perhaps it has never worked right except in the rarest cases. And a broken system can only replicate itself. As Bohm states, only the power of consciousness can put a disordered brain into order.

This reordering is the function of the Guru, the Holy Spirit or power of wholeness. The Guru function is largely remedial. It arcs the gaps left in our development; both injects into our brains an experience of maturity and brings enough order for development to resume. The awakening of Shakti through initiation is the equivalent of a surgical operation to restore eyesight. But most of us have been blind since birth, and must rebuild, slowly and carefully, our entire conceptual system to include this new light.

The awakening of Shakti in Siddha Yoga initiation is often explosively joyous, followed by a less spectacular but highly effective quiet development. The same initial exuberance can break loose at any time, though, in the ongoing development which Shakti brings about. Peter Mann, an accountant from Melbourne, shared the following after an intensive with Muktananda in December 1979:

"During the intensive, Baba came around and gave the touch. I fell into a deep meditation and realized that in my meetings with Baba over the last six years a part of me meets him for the first time, and another part of me has never been separate from him. On the one hand, the relationship is ever new and on the other hand totally eternal—so vast is the connection between the guru and the disciple.

"This thought was followed by myself performing spontaneous *bastrika* [a rapid yogic breathing which leads to suspension of thought], which acted like an ignition force and I found myself soaring through a mass of blue light. I felt as though I was in a cosmic rocket ship which was moving at such an incredible speed that it had no structure. Beautiful blue patterns and geometrical designs unfolded all about me.

"Eventually I came to a halt in front of a wall of white light and the bastrika started again. My energy became completely centered and acted like a laser which bored into the wall and burst through to the other side. I was amazed to find myself being pushed backward by a force on the other side. It was a wonderful experience. I completely gave up the idea of reaching somewhere, and allowed the force to move me at will. I felt like a leaf falling from a tree riding on the current of the wind. Then the bastrika started again and my legs locked and my whole being stood firm against the light and it started to stream right through me. Then it was more than just light. There were galaxies of stars, planets, and celestial beings all moving back and forth through me. Then the stars started to explode, planets were splitting in two, and celestial beings disintegrating. This cosmic process of creation and destruction was taking place all around me. I remain untouched in the serene state of the ever watchful One."

Peter's experience is far more than the equivalent of a psychedelic trip without drugs. His experience is development of the ability to move into highly creative states, and it is a great learning of what the cosmic process is about. And his final state of the ever watchful One is, of course, an experience of the fourth and final state of development, Reversibility Thinking, insight-intelligence, the witness state.

"Play on the surface" is the best description of what the movement toward maturity is supposed to be, and the only way true play can be allowed is to let the *work* be done for us by the holonomic order itself. The creation and separation of a unique personality out of this unity is hardly an error, nor a dirty trick of fate, nor something to be overcome. It is the developmental way to create a creator. Muktananda states that to be given human life is an incredible gift.

Separation for relationship is the key of life. Siddha Yoga is joyful for me because it re-establishes the play of relationship. Kashmir Shaivism, an ancient Scripture from Northern India, on which Muktananda draws, sees life as Shiva (peace, insight, and intelligence) separating from his lover, Shakti (energy, power, exuberance, and action) in order to relate with her. And in their eternal-instantaneous separation and union, all creation—the whole explicate, implicate, and causal realms—springs into being, which is, surely, an eternal explosion of joy.

VII .

Form and Content

Plato's ". . . supremely suggestive and fertilizing quality . . ." writes Northrop Frye, "lies in the fact that he was the only philosopher who was artist enough to master a visionary form, and hence . . . [could] suggest an infinity of responses instead of compelling a single one."

Child-rearing should offer an infinity of responses while demanding few, if any, specific responses—which is to say, culture should be a visionary balance of form and content. Form tends to restrict even as it brings content into being, and content seems to chafe at the bit of any restriction even though it must have form to be expressed. But these tendencies are from imbalance, a lack of artistic skill. Form out of balance is stasis and death, constricting content. Content out of balance is chaos, destroying form, its channel for realization.

A formal structure is a discipline. Ideally, form would be a flexible and open-ended process for shaping and supporting content. Form and content should function together like mother and newborn infant at bonding-time; each should furnish the other with the appropriate stimuli for bonding; each should be the key that unlocks the other's response.

The child, as a new content, continually signals his needs for formal structuring and screens his environment for the expected response to his needs. Should that response fail, he sinks into apathy. The unresponsive parent, like the devouring mother, indicates imbalance; like the rebellious child, she indicates a genetic system gone awry, one that expresses conditioning, not nature; something molded not created.

Both society's failure to respond to our needs and our corresponding antisocial acts indicate the unnatural. Form should be in love with content and vice versa, since each is really the other, their division only an assumption made for creative play. We should bond to our society at a point of our maturation, as we did with our parents (or should have). But the later bonding's success depends upon the earlier one. Bonding is the power that molds form and content into a unified work. Bonding must be developed—or allowed to develop. Once developed, anything can be bonded, any experience molded into a unified work.

Chaos is the unknown, that implicate-causal energy which awaits being ordered into meaning and perceptual experience. The taboos of social control are usually prompted and perpetuated by anxiety over the unknown. Taboo may indicate a lack of ability to lift order out of chaos. A child brought up to maintain a taboo system, rather than create, doesn't learn to order the unknown into perceptual experience, and will be anxious over the unknown in turn. The unknown is rightly interpreted as the chaos that occurs should meaning and order break down. Through anxiety, however, meaning and order are projected onto a fixed outer system, rather than recognized as an inner ability of our mind/brain to bond into an orderly unit the disparate elements of potential.

Intelligence is the ability to interact with possibility and "lift things into order." This takes a certain daring (which is why intelligence and confidence are almost synonymous). There is no anxiety when a developed, creative person sees chaos as the raw material for his own work of art, the art of creative perception. A developed or mature person should be able to create a form corresponding to the content of his creative desire, and culture should provide for development of this ability.

A culture should automatically become obsolescent as its people-products mature. The successful parent is one whose child matures to walk away without a backward glance. Backward glances, either of obsessive love or hatred, show incomplete development, looking back to pick up missing pieces, to try and patch a broken system.

Sonata-allegro form is an abstraction that has existence only in application, only as it gives shape to sound. Applied by a genius, the form dissolves into the content which it shapes, and its shape is unnoticeable. Applied by mediocrity, the form determines the content; rather than suggesting an infinity of response, it has compelled a single one. The form is then noticeable, like bones sticking out of flesh and marring the shape (as in Mozart's pseudosymphony, *The Musical Joke*).

Ability is form and creative imagination is content. Creative imagination is thought married to insight. The human is a form for content. When the form is considered the content, life leaves that form. When we identify with our body and brain, our possibility as a form for content is crippled and we end without content—truly hollow men. The world is the "larger body of man," a source of content out of which formal devices can be constructed, allowing for ever greater realms of form to give life to ever greater realms of content. When our larger body is considered a preset, ready-made *matter,* rather than the materials out of which new form and content can arise, we sink into tyranny.

When culture as life's form freezes into tyranny, it regenerates its own form, rather than continually finding new form according to life's fluid, ongoing needs. So nothing produced within a tyrannical culture can deliver that culture from its tyranny. (We see each salvation-brimming demagogue rushing down to "clean up the mess in Washington," only to clutter it more as he lines his pockets.) We think of freedom as absence of tyranny—yet every move for such a freedom ends as a tighter tyranny. A first step toward freedom is to see it as the ability to create (not as absence of tyranny).

Ability is developmental. A static system conditions us to maintain that system, and system-maintenance constricts development to those abilities necessary to that system. Constricting development creates anxiety which promotes the static system. Anxiety-ridden parents automatically model anxiety for their children, who have no choice but to mirror that anxiety.

So, once fallen into anxiety, a species can't raise itself. When our perception develops out of tyranny, we are fixed into a limited world and determined by the things we see. Determined by our cultural environment, we either maintain the fixity of it, no matter how awful it is, in fear of losing the little we have, or we try to engineer it mechanically, trying to make things in our head come out right.

"If the doors of perception were cleansed," Blake claimed, "every thing would appear to man as it is, infinite." Neither form nor content exist as fixed items, but as events for and of perception. When the doors of perception are cleansed, the world of frozen matter bursts and all is fluid and free. Consider, for instance, the Shaktipat experience of Rudrani Farbman, of New York City, who, in 1974, took an intensive with Muktananda:

Baba pinched her hard on the forehead between her eyes. She felt: ". . . a sudden indrawing of energy, a consolidation of strength . . . then majestic, free of self-doubts." Riding her bicycle home that afternoon, everything ". . . began to turn into a sea of seething energy, taking form slowly and fluidly like slow waves in the ocean. Forms rolled and churned like cellular life, snakelike, extraplanetary." Rudrani began to see that the forms were ". . . tiny scintillating blue dots . . . dazzlingly beautiful. Everything sparkled, caught up in this radiance of dots. Forms dissolved . . . now all was dots." She became immersed in this ocean of blue dots which gave ecstasy and peace.

"So this was what it all was, and always was," she thought. "Why had I not been told?" (Indeed, why haven't we all been told? But who has there been to tell us?) "I began to play with it," she goes on; she would focus and buildings and people emerged; relaxed and all merged into blue dots and ecstasy. She knew then that it was up to her to either keep an arbitrary world together or let it go. Nothing was the same after this. Anxiety dropped away; she became fluid and free herself, her relations with her world changing.

Perception, like thought, is an end-product. We, as perceivers, are recipients of that product. Thinking can't change the mechanics of our thought or perception any more than we can, by taking thought, increase our stature by a cubit. No thought generated by any brain in error can do other than replicate that error. Only insight can change the workings of a disordered brain. If the capacity for insight is lost to culture, that capacity must be given back from a source outside that culture or from a person plugged into a different circuitry, that is, a genius beyond the circle of that norm.

Rudrani's experience was a form of insight, a revelation which, like Einstein's brief flash, forever changed the landscape of her mind. Insight is given; it can be a grace; but the nature of the insight, and thus whatever change it brings, is determined by the nature of the passion and will generating that revelation. Insight is a form for content and the source of new content. It is a function which can give rise to anything. The determinate is our will and what we are after. We reap as we sow.

There is a way in which subtle and physical energies can become mutually determinate and interact back and forth. The Gospels state that what we loose on earth is loosed in heaven and what is loosed in heaven is loosed on earth. The discipline of a form influences the nature of the content it shapes; just as the content influences the shape of the formal discipline it needs to be expressed as experience. A scientific discipline produces the content its form generates, but that content to be generated influences its needed formal discipline. The passion of the scientist's search enters into the shape of his discovery—even when that passion is generated by a longing for a Nobel prize. We naturally assume that that which is then discovered has "always been there," but mind's creative act of form and content has brought it into our experience. Assuming it "always there" is one way we lose ourself to our own creation. We cast our gold into the fire of the mind, create a golden calf, fall down and worship it as something separate from and greater than our own capacity, become eccentric and thereby mad. Muktananda says: "You create your own illusion, and become entangled in it."

This was the insight given Rudrani. She was a hatha yoga teacher. She wanted to bring about health and wholeness in herself and her students. Her insight given was into the bond of power and creation itself. Though her techniques had been bootstrap, her mind had been opened and readied for illumination when it came. And it came not from her self-generating efforts, but from the bond of power responding to her efforts. If we persist long enough, insight will break into our system and cleanse the doors of our perception. Then we may see the world as content for our mind's formative play, as material for creativity rather than the frozen matter of economics.

Einstein's insight was into the binding energy of matter, and now we have atomic proliferation and the terrors of atomic annihilation. Kekulé's postulate has brought down upon us the terrors of a chemical world in pollution. Insight itself is surely not grace, though it is a form for *possible* grace. Insight is our only vehicle for change, but the nature of that change depends upon the nature of our will and passion. Ultimately, the answers we receive depend on the questions that we ask. What irony that the insights which bring terror and destruction on us are hailed as milestones of progress; while an insight which united heaven and earth in Rudrani should be so silent and unsung.

VIII

The Error-Correction Error

Nature uses a purposive randomness in development, to allow for an infinite number of variables. Watch a child learning to walk, a wobbly process filled with a myriad of minor mishaps. The motor center's plan of action pays no attention to wobbles and fumbles; its blueprint impels the child to hop up and try again indefinitely. Nature's plan is a flexible design for a specific goal; a course of action where course means form and action means content. The haphazard wobbly movement is the content which the form of intent gradually shapes into the art of walking.

While sailing against the wind we must tack, zigzagging to maintain a straight-line course. Each zig and zag moves away from the compass line, yet maintains the course. We navigate by constant course-correction.

In modern chemotherapy, the course of correction is less precise. The medicine man injects a potion of chemicals into a sick body to exorcise a disease. Often the victim's body reacts poorly to the chemical while the disease is untouched. To offset the ill effects of the first chemical, the medicine man injects yet another chemical. This counteraction often brings on further reaction which calls for even greater counteractions. Finally, the cryptic notice is scribbled on the "progress chart": "Died of complications."

We consider the bugs that feed on our plants an error needing our correction. We introduce a host of deadly chemicals to correct those bugs. Now the injection of chemicals into the body of the Earth reaches massive proportions, creating problems on an as yet uncomprehended scale. The bugs are coming back stronger than ever, while the cryptic notice is scribbled on the ecological progress chart: "Dying of complications."

In Chapter VI, I touched on a biological plan of magnificent proportions, a straight-line course of development that is built into our genes. The plan is flexible, to accommodate an infinite number of variables, while its goal is specific and clear: a way for creating a new hologram out of the holonomic movement, a new representative of the whole; a new creator out of the creation. The plan is a way to develop thought out of consciousness as a tool of insight-intelligence. The plan depends on developing ability, which encompasses a certain amount of trial and error. In fact, the biological plan can accommodate error easily since error is only an aspect of experience, or the content that gives the form life.

Something happened to this grand plan, though, perhaps historically, and the happening is repeated anew in each of us. In the course of implementing the plan, we stumble occasionally, as is natural and to be expected. But we do not, as is natural and to be expected, correct our course. That is, we don't immediately follow our intent and maintain our alignment with our plan. We become engrossed in the nature of our stumble, our error of the moment, and try to correct the error instead of our course. And at this point we Fall.[1]

Development is learning to walk this straight-line system built into us. As is natural to any skill, our walking is crude at first. We wobble about, stumble and fall. The wobbles and falls are incidental so long as we keep our eye on that straight line of development—so long as we stay aligned. Everything unfolds in its good time when we do that and wobbles and wide excursions amount to nothing.

The Fall takes place when we pay attention to the wobble and not our course; when we notice the wobble as a wobble, an isolated fact of its own; when we take our eyes off our straight-line course and shift our attention to the fact of our wobble. When we do that, we immediately feel anxious over our error, which we see not as course-deviation but as self-contained. Our anxiety is over being off-course, having shifted focus to the error, but we *interpret* our anxiety as over having made an error.

So long as we are in line with our biological plan, everything is right—including wobbles and stumbles. Jean Liedloff speaks of the "in-arms" period of infancy. When the infant is in the mother's arms, everything is right and nothing much can go wrong. When "out-of-arms," or in abandonment, nothing is right and everything goes wrong. The one main signal of need is not being met and none of the other signals then work. When we are in-arms biologically, development is smooth, playful, fairly effortless, and all energies remain coordinated. When we are out-of-arms biologically, uneasiness immediately sets in since the body and brain are looking for cues and responses expected from millions of years of development, and not getting them. Processes go out of synchrony and internal conflict begins to pile up. We fall into anxiety over our error and are impelled to correct that error.

In trying to correct our error, we have to take our eyes off our course of development and concentrate on the error. Then several things happen. For one thing, we are now off-course, going in a direction counter to our development. Our error has become our direction, and our pseudocourse. The error is not developmental of itself and the direction of error only leads to itself. We have stopped our growth in mid-wobble.

At this point, thought becomes detached from consciousness and insight-intelligence, which *are* the straight-line course. Thought tries to become self-sufficient of necessity, which is to say, thought in error tries to correct itself, rather than align itself again with the course of development. (Which course can, as said before, contain a multitude of errors with grace and ease, while the error can in no way contain or even refer to the course.)

When anxiety arises as some thought in our mind, the "pressure" of it (to use David Bohm's term) immediately breeds another thought to try and ease that pressure. The novelty effect of each new thought brings us the feeling of some momentary relief of our anxiety, only to find anxiety immediately reinstated, inherent within that relieving thought—which calls for another. Anxiety can only breed anxiety. Anxiety is the one condition intolerable to us, and thought generated by anxiety—even though the impulse is generated to *escape* anxiety—will always relate to, and have inherent within it, that anxiety. Isolated thinking can't give unity, and only in unity are we free of anxiety.

When in sailing against the wind we shift our tack, we are guided by our course-direction. In the error-correction error, *we change the compass setting itself* away from its original goal over to the direction the *error is going in.*

With the wrong compass setting, everything starts going wrong and we are besieged by errors demanding correction. The problem with correcting error is that we become what we behold. With our eye on our course of development, it is impossible, regardless of context, to be off-course. Regardless of how wildly we veer off or how complex and unruly the variables become, we are always on-course and everything is all right, when our eye is on the course. Our true course encompasses everything conceivable. When our compass is set correctly, and we know our relation to it, we can pile into choppy waters without qualm. The same arena of experience can be positive or negative according to our alignment or lack of it. Course-alignment lifts order out of chaos. When our eye is on the error, though, we become that error. And like attracts like. Error produces error. When chaos is our orientation, we can't lift anything into order.

The brain is designed to correlate its information and ability around and amplify whatever cues are provided it for action. When error is the brain's concentration, no matter what materials it correlates and relates in its "corrections," the brain's processes center on the error—they serve it. When error is the basis of brain action, error is always inherent within the product of that brain. Bake with salt instead of sugar and you won't get a sweet cake.

Error-correction can arouse in us that passionate intensity which will eventually initiate an insight-revelation—as witness science and technology—and that response, from the enormous power of the creative realm itself, will be in keeping with the materials of the error. The error-position will be strengthened while giving the outer, temporary appearance of being correction.

All the negative numbers in the world will not add up to a single positive one—although an unlimited negative-mathematics could be constructed. Thought, once become self-generative, can only reproduce itself and maintain its disorder. Only insight can reorder and bring the brain's responses into alignment with the whole.

In our flush of congratulatory excitement over having corrected an error, we don't notice that the solution is only a varied form of the error or a worse error in disguise (that the DDT might be more destructive than the grasshopper). Eventually we notice, though, to our general dismay, that there are errors here we hadn't noticed before; not noticing that the new errors are simply by-products of the old, briefly camouflaged as correction. So we set out anew to correct these new problems besetting us.

So error proliferates; each error breeds new ones like a tree that branches at every tip. (This is the bureaucracy-Pentagon syndrome.) Anxiety drives us to try and patch up each error and we fall further behind until, locked as we are in the "magnitude of the problems facing our day," even the notion of development, a biological plan, of a meaning and goal to life, is lost to us. Lost in our maze of ever-multiplying error, we begin to consider ourselves the "error-correction beast," or the "problem-solving animal," and think of life itself as error. We think the real nature of humanity is this vast sprawling bag of worms called society and its ills, and really believe the nature of the mind/brain is to try and solve that wriggling mess.

Culture can't possibly be the vehicle for implementing the developmental plan when caught in error-correction. It becomes a taboo system of prediction and control, trying to organize the machinery for error-correction. Development is then bent toward a prediction and control which violates every facet of nature's design. With prediction and control the reigning passion and anxiety the normal state, the bulk of our energy goes to solve problems that continually outstrip us.

Under the pressure of such anxiety, the brain system can make no movement not related to that anxiety. Every effort will be toward removing the *cause* of the anxiety, which is interpreted, of course, as caused by all the unsolved errors. This anxiety-orientation automatically isolates us from our source of power, our consciousness and insight, which alone can remove anxiety.

Prolonged anxiety results in arrogance, our conviction not that our thought is necessarily self-sufficient, but that isolated thought is all we have, all we are; that we must simply bluster through as best we can, head held high, bloodied but unbowed; our only criterion a kind of shifting consensus on the nature of our isolation.

The solution, of course, appears as *no* solution. The solution is to turn our eyes away from the mass of errors screaming for correction and learn again to focus on the goal of development, that straight, simple line of the biological plan. The solution is to open to insight-intelligence, admit to our thought's absolute insufficiency, and allow our thought to be used as the instrument of the holonomic order within our head—as designed.

Now isolated thought, locked in its arrogant posture of prediction and control, fears the unknown, which always means the insight-intelligence realm. But, once the shift is made from error-correction to realignment with the plan, *error isn't something to correct anymore.* (How this baffled me!) Error is again only a deviation from the course, and the course is immediately the focal point of attention again. Course-correction then replaces error-correction and then all that exists is the plan and its execution, which can encompass a multitude of errors.

To isolated and arrogant thought, emerging from a brain locked into escape from anxiety, such an observation is sheer gibberish. And strangely, such a simple turning maneuver is the prime sin against an error-correction society. One should devote one's life to mankind, give one's self for the welfare of others; live for the good of the whole of man (be general but never specific, abstract but never concrete). Not to do so is to be selfish, a shameful state. The sound commonsense logic of this cultural imperative cloaks the fact that the only way to live for others in the way held forth is to devote one's life to error-correction; join in the great forward march of progress under the party of your choice; solve technology's problems for a better tomorrow; better things for better living through chemistry, and so on. All of which means accept thought as the totality and deny the whole mind/brain function as possible.

So it is that our society, and the new "monoculture" of technology sweeping the globe like a cancer, is an error-correction system in which nothing ever works—at least for long. Everything always fails—everything. (How angry this observation makes the believers in error-correction and progress.) Every solution heaps failure higher around us, as our leaders (those most successful in promising error-correction) exhort us to greater effort.

The registered voter is the model, as yesterday's Great Political Plan tumbles to today's embarrassing fiasco and tomorrow's bitter recriminations.

Nothing *works*. Everything touched by error-correction turns to dust and ashes. And in the great clamor of fault-finding and lust for scapegoat blood, the insanity of the system goes untouched and unnoticed. Thought out of alignment cannot produce, generate, discover, or make one single product free of eventual destructiveness. Every single "great discovery" sooner or later turns into nightmare. The few moments of truth and beauty cropping up within an error-correction culture do so in spite of that culture. The rare Bach, Blake, or Bartók are bought at the price of a grim struggle, not to create, but to be free to do so. Ironically, their rare achievements are hailed as and attributed to, culture.

Every saint and genius has told us two things: we are not guilty of error nor called on to correct it; and the plan of life is built into us and its truth can never be removed. That truth in us can only be covered over, and that truth is our ever-present alignment with the whole; the truth of our real Self is God Himself, the perfection of our *own* divine being.

How the priests of culture hate this notion. How it embarrasses and threatens them, for their positions are founded on and maintained by error. To suggest that error doesn't really exist or need correction is to suggest their identity doesn't exist, that the outer shell of their allegiance is a fraud. To suggest that error should not be corrected strips them of the motivation of others, of their meaning, drive, ambition, purpose, They must, in fact, keep error going or be out of a job, just as the medicine man must breed illness or find no market for his nostrums. Nothing so disturbs the policeman as the idea of man as essentially honest—no calamity would be so great as an absence of crime. The Pentagonian insists that human nature is warlike since any other position would disarm him. Were education to work, were children actually led forth to knowledge, educators would immediately disappear. Take away prediction and control, and bureaucracy would collapse. Take away separation from God, and the churches would empty.

In my early days of Siddha Yoga, I was often irritated that Muktananda seemed oblivious to the social crimes against humanity erupting all about us. Baba's presence itself had to bring about in me (by osmosis, I suppose) enough strength of mind, a certain clearing of error in my brain, for me to understand that he is not blind and deaf to the misery and terror about us. (Quite the contrary, only compassion could induce him to put up with our nonsense.) He sees the misery well enough, but only by a shift of viewpoint, an effort of unfocusing, perhaps. Otherwise he sees through error to the truth, which truth is our actual identity with God and perfection in Him. For truth can only see truth, it can't see error as legitimate fact. I wanted Baba to join with me in "getting those rascals" perpetrating these crimes. (And I certainly had my list, with medicine men at the top.) But Baba would have none of my craziness. He didn't even catch my fuzzy wavelength. I was asking him, in effect, to join me in error-correction. He invited me, on the other hand, to join him in truth.

The power of the error-correction error should never be underestimated, though, for it both controls and constitutes the world of folly (and our very program of brain until the grace of insight breaks us free). A nation of 220 million psyches locked into the anxiety of error-correction is no small force. The gauge of the men of spirit can be found, in fact, in their response to this negativity. I recall during the Vietnam war (my protests futile, my personal anguish at the breaking point) how infuriated I was with a priest-friend who refused to join my march on the Capitol. He preached only that we turn to God, and I thought him evasive and weak. I know now that the attempt to revive the Christian Church in the 1960's failed not from the "death of God" nonsense of precious professors desperate for publication so much as from the social-activism, secular-city nonsense of arrogant professors who failed to understand why Jesus was indifferent to Rome but wrathful over the Pharisees of the state church.

Some of the would-be Gurus imported from the East fall into the error-correction error (which operates like a giant black hole in space, sucking all light into it). For instance, I was honored with an award by a famous international meditation mail-order house (of Eastern origins). The walls of the meditation center were covered with graphs showing the effects of meditation on physical processes (correcting blood pressure, brain waves, and so on). Even more graphically displayed and boasted, were charts showing the statistical effects of meditation on current social ills. A 2-percent reduction of rape in Racine, plunder in Paris, bank robbery in Brooklyn, were all attributed to groups of meditators in various parts of the world. Even the President's historic firing of his Cabinet in 1979 was attributed to meditation influencers. Whether these attributions were valid is beside the point; the attempt by the meditators to correct social ills shows that they were perpetuating the error-correction error.

The absolute and final arrogance of ego is in playing the secret power behind the scenes. Muktananda, like Jesus, could never be seduced by error-correction, for one in truth sees error as illusion. (How this notion baffled and irritated me when I first encountered it!) Error is illusion because for it to be real, it must be aligned with the holonomic order. Were it aligned, it would be true and not an error (to form a tautology which, though naive, is true). Error is misalignment or disorder.

Through the grace of Siddha Yoga, we can deprogram this error indoctrination and shift from error-correction to course-alignment. Through the modeling given us in our great beings, we find that by turning back to a course-alignment, a *navigator* is here within us, and a navigation system which, like a gyroscope of universal power, simply never deviates from course. Perhaps this course is culture as it should be, a magnificent form for the infinitely varied content our life of learning should unfold. The only action such a culture would impel is that we keep our eye on our course, which requires a certain discipline and attentiveness, but which can then suggest and encompass an infinity of response.

Any error can be cut through, and the course maintained, with this navigator within us in charge. He is the bonding-force connecting us with the totality of our life. Our navigator is the spirit of our life, and spiritual growth is developing all the navigational instruments needed for life's venture. This ability should unfold and develop from birth, but it gets sidetracked through anxiety-enculturation and goes largely dormant. The dynamic awakening which Muktananda brings about is the navigator himself, our "secret twin" always suspected within, our other half, leaping in where he has belonged all along, to start getting the ship back on-course.

Awakening us to our course and this navigator within is Muktananda's task. He evokes that within us and guides our development through instruction and modeling. Through this grace and guidance, error fades as the focus of our life, while this infinitely open play of course-alignment takes over, a play that has the universe itself as its field.

IX

The Great Vaccination

The archetype of Western culture is undeniably the Bible and its derivatives. It provided the motives for our major art, architecture, and philosophy for nineteen hundred years and brought about the peculiar split of mind called The Enlightenment, which ushered in science and technology.

The Old Testament's "raving Jehova" is, as Northrop Frye expressed it: " . . . when one gives up the attempt to extract a unified moral code out of [it] . . . a profoundly true vision of a false god."

As so often with genius, Jesus was at a radical discontinuity with his background. (Attempts to "unify" the four Gospels with the Old Testament led to a hilarious logic.) If Jesus's "good news" of our identity with God and freedom from guilt were accepted, it would automatically abolish tyranny. To be free of guilt and at one with the universal system is to be free of anxiety—and you can threaten and control a man only through his anxiety. So the forces of social-political control must always induce and maintain that anxiety.

After a bit of floundering, tyranny absorbed and utilized Jesus's good news by inverting it. Jesus had tried to make himself "transparent" to his Gospel; to point only toward the function of wholeness within us, and prevent people from projecting their need onto him instead of turning to their own source of power. All tyranny had to do was deify him, make him "opaque"—a target *for* mass projection of inner need. This both relieves social pressure and directs it into controllable channels.

Instead of proclaiming our freedom from guilt, Jesus was held to be the only human in history free of guilt. His equation of the God-Man Unity was turned into a historical event as well: God was allowed to have been man only once in history, in the person of Jesus. The "Father who gives only good and perfect gifts" reverted back to Jehova. No longer was there "The Father within" who does wonderful things, but *Old Nobodaddy,* as Blake called Him, *nobody's father,* a tyrant more ghastly than the worst of the Old Testament, since removed completely from the universe, remote and unavailable; whose "horror at our impurity" impelled him to engineer the murder of his "only begotten son" to appease his own wrath; who yet remained ready to toss us into an eternal hell-fire for our inherited, inevitable, and inescapable sin, unless His son somehow intervened. (And this bizarre, illogical nightmare held the attention of some of the best minds of the West for nearly two millennia.)

The central point of history (and history may be a fiction largely originating from Christendom) was fixed as this one-shot occurrence of God as man in Jesus, and the primal heresy of *all* history—the sin of all ages—was to consider the God-Man equation possible again, in some other person, least of all one's own miserable person. Man was cut off from God by an absolute gulf, bridgeable only by Jesus, who was absolutely owned by the forces of social-political control. His possible grace was dispensed piecemeal through sacraments, at a price. Between condemned man and aloof God stood the state church, selling salvation-someday-maybe, after death, in return for now-support of the state, throughout life. The neatest double bind ever invented.

You might think this a quaint antiquity with no bearing on thought today—but we carry the direct imprint of this heresy in the whole fabric of modern life. For instance, one evening not too long ago, I was at home, reading about *Hamsa* meditation, my daughter doing schoolwork at a table some three feet to my right. I had been doing *Hamsa* meditation for months, inwardly saying *Ham* (hah-m) on the in-breath, *sa* (sah) on the out-breath. I realized how I had avoided the literal translation of *Hamsa*: I am That, because it literally means: I am God. It isn't that such a statement is heresy or anathema: more effectively, it is in bad taste, rather an embarrassment in our culture—perhaps vulgar.

An argument ensued in my head. My other-voice (always arguing with me) said: "Say the words, fool, you've been saying 'I am God' in Sanskrit for months." But I really couldn't make myself say the embarrassing phrase, in spite of my intellectual smile over my own nonsense. The argument grew serious, though, and finally my other-me inwardly shouted: "Just say the phrase, idiot, say 'I am God—I am God!' " Feeling foolish, I threw restraint to the wind and inwardly said: "Okay—so I am God!"

Instantly, without warning, open-eyed looking out at the room, on saying the words, I was pulled out of my body, as though the "real me" were rubber inside a casement. I came out from every nook and cranny, hard and fast, through the back of my neck—and found myself free above my body. Shock waves of ecstasy then consumed me and I was "lifted up"—as though at the speed of light—into a peace quite beyond my understanding, an area of my being beyond words and descriptions. I came back into my body as I had gone out, and my daughter was not aware that I had undergone an inner-world earthquake.

According to Siddha Yoga, I had "broken through a block," this one an inherited block of *heresy* or taboo of considerable power. I had again glimpsed that *something* within myself against which I had been inoculated.

We vaccinate, you know, by injecting into our body dead or near-dead virus that cause a disease. Our body's defense system easily routes such a weak enemy, and, having learned that particular martial maneuver, can repeat the performance with ease and skill when the real enemy comes along. Great encounters of life and death can then take place below the level of our awareness.

In just this way, heresy concerning the "central point in history" proved the most potent vaccine in history. Most early religious education is a vaccination of classical proportions. We are injected with a dead or nearly dead form of the actual disease (the disease of

God, this is) from an early age. I remember, at age twelve, being the hottest acolyte in our Episcopal diocese that diocese offered to send me to the most prestigious boys' prep school in the South, to be followed, if all went well, with the university and maybe, of course, the seminary for Episcopal priests after that. I was elated, my mother horrified. "All nice people go to church," she clipped, as she nixed the deal, "but they don't let it go to their heads."

She need not have been overly concerned. Once inoculated, our system throws the real thing out every time it tries to assert itself anyway (and the clerical collar changes only the semantics of the vaccination). That disease never spreads so far as the head, much less the heart—where the real action takes place.

Our vaccination is against the most natural of all functions, our spirit. The word *spirit,* though, is almost meaningless, either over-filled with useless connotations or stripped and barren. Spirit is Shakti, energy, the particular aspect of energy that bonds together, that connects, that lifts order out of chaos as a unit in unity, with the whole of things. In the New Testament, the "Holy Spirit" was the energy or power that came with wholeness of self. Jesus spoke of the "Holy Comforter." *Holy* means wholeness (nothing more esoteric), and *comfort* means with strength, or from strength, the power or strength that comes from being united.

Our vaccination, then, is against the bonding-force within us, that design of nature which molds the disparate functions of body, brain, mind, personality, and so on, into a coherent whole in harmony with the larger whole. A lack of spiritual development means that thought gets isolated from insight-intelligence and consciousness. A need for spiritual guidance means a need for restoring wholeness between thought and insight-intelligence, which can only take place through the power of consciousness.

Spiritual guidance can only be "revealed," as a result; it is of the same stuff as insight and can only "arrive full-blown in the brain," not be computed or originated by that brain. It is against the insight function that we have been vaccinated. (That may be why we must make such enormous efforts to trigger insight-response along any line.) Thought is designed to be only a part of our awareness-existence. Consciousness and insight-intelligence should be equal or superior portions of our perception. Isolated in our thought, we are seldom conscious and only very rarely experience insight. Were the "disease of God" against which we are now vaccinated allowed to unfold within us as designed, our full maturity would be that state which is now either denied or projected outside ourselves as something remote and unattainable.

This is not to claim that there is a "natural religion" which would grow unfettered were it allowed, for no capacity is natural in the sense that it will flower unattended or appear miraculously fully developed. All functions, including the overall function of coordinating wholeness, or spirit, must follow the law of development. A corresponding stimulus must be given from without, from a developed capacity of the same order, to start development; and an ongoing developmental model must be given with a proper nurturing to sustain growth; the logical stages of growth must be honored, we must be allowed to crawl before we walk.

This need for a living model of wholeness is a qualification which nullifies most religions, and nearly every preacher, priest, guru, or holy man going. Wholeness means absolute unity, not almost—just as you can't be "just a little bit pregnant," you can't be almost whole and model wholeness. Cant, dogma, theory, spiritual exhortation, philosophy, and so on are general expressions of the arrogance of isolated thought trying to create a semantic world that will be whole. Even piety, good intentions, and earnestness can never, alone, develop the process within us called the Spirit. Development must have awakening and modeling by a person who exemplifies that which must be evoked from within.

Our children do mirror us, as they must, as we mirrored our parents, and had to. Each next generation proves anxiety-ridden, half-mad, antisocial, depressed idiots, drowning themselves in alcohol and "disappointing" our hopes that this time it might all be different. By our fruits, we should recognize our state. We reap as we sow and as was sowed for us. Mind-in-here mirrors its world-out-there, we become what we behold.

I mentioned a Shakti experience which led to my direct meeting with Muktananda. I was reading Baba's little book, *Siddha Meditation,* one evening, dropped off to sleep, awoke with a bright light shining in my eyes, opened them, and was startled to see a beautiful white marble statue of the head of Jesus directly in front of me. The eyes of the statue were real, however, and beckoned me to go into meditation. Even as I closed my eyes for meditation, I felt the hard nose of the statue bump against my face, and the statue started *breathing* into my nostrils—a bizarre action I had never (at that time) heard of. (It's one of the ways Muktananda gives Shaktipat.) The breath didn't stop coming in, though; it filled me and continued until, it seemed, I had breathed in the whole universe. Those great waves of ecstatic joy started coursing up through my body as I was lifted up into realms of being beyond description.

For five decades, I had wrestled with spirit in the vague, abstract semantic form of my inoculation, investing my energy in this search and getting only my own energy, slightly worn, back. My romantic idealism and emotional-sentimental love projected onto the figure of Jesus (my only model) was reflected back into my life as romantic idealism and emotional-sentimental "love," but not as the power and transformation I so needed. The live and real spirit, however, once I had been exposed to it, moved into my life *through* the very symbols of my vaccination.

A young Catholic woman took an intensive with us in 1979. Baba "gave her the touch" and she fell into meditation. She had a clear vision of the Virgin Mary coming to her—beautiful, warm, loving. The young woman reached out, in her vision, to embrace the Virgin—but, of all things, Muktananda entered the vision, picked up the Virgin, tucked her under his arm, and walked off with her. At which point, the young woman saw that the Virgin had been only a plaster statue.

Statues are fine reminders for those already given the life of spirit, but only life can bestow life. Jesus said, "God is a God of the living, not of the dead."

Nor does an agnostic or atheistic upbringing give a nice clean slate, ready for some "truth" to be written on it. Belief and unbelief are semantic niceties, having no more to do with the cultural effect of vaccination than the political facades of Democrat-Republican have to do with the machinations of social control.

Inoculated against inner unity, we develop the true disease of alienation, which is separation from our Self. Cut off from our bonding-power in childhood, we spend our lives buying facsimiles of it in hopes of recovering something we know we have lost. Tyranny exists through threat, which exists as a play on our anxiety, which tyranny perpetuates. As Frye put it: " . . . a God whose interests do not run counter to those of man cannot be invoked in support of a tyranny. [Thus] . . . it is in the God of official Christianity . . . invented as a homeopathic cure for the teachings of Jesus, that state religion has produced its masterpiece."

The God within, toward which Jesus pointed, though historically projected out again as unattainable, is our inner process of development, our full and perfect maturation as designed; thought perfected as an instrument of insight-intelligence and open to the power of consciousness. "Be ye perfect as your Father in Heaven is perfect" was not some cruel jest, but a simple observation of what life is about. Perfection is full development, not some divine abstraction of essence or quality removed from reality. Christendom made of perfection a state devoid of humanness and so unattainable to us humans—which automatically creates guilt in us over our automatic and assured failure.

Muktananda insists that our perfection is already achieved, always present right here in us, that our job is to realize our true state—which means to push past our vaccination (rather as St. Francis overcoming his greatest horror and kissing the leper fully on the lips—at which point all the bells of heaven rang).

The god of the Enlightenment period was a glorification of thought as self-sufficient, thus totally arrogant; a "perfection" which eschewed all human traits and became the impersonal power, a mathematical function, of a clockwork, mechanical universe. The followers of such a god produced, as Frye notes: " . . . men of destiny; men of force or cunning rather than intelligence or imagination." Cunning truly expresses the history of the kings and rulers battening on each other's blood; explorers and conquerors, industrialists and exploiters, bureaucrats and Pentagonians; the hoodlums and whores, filling our textbooks and newspapers as heroes and heroines; right down into our technological machine men, exemplars of impersonal power at remote control; who substitute computers for thinking, build atomic bombs delivered by mathematical calculations, and talk through electronic gadgetry of going to the stars. Our split-mind projected wholeness onto a clockwork mechanical god-out-there, built machines to try and replace our corresponding loss of personal power, and we lost our identity to our own machinery.

As we project our longing for our whole Self onto something out there in "reality," we project our resulting inner terror and anxiety onto our social world. And the unforgivable sin of Western thought has been to break this double-projection, since the illusion of our whole world of folly would then snap, and its reigning priesthood collapse.

Science, as the new priesthood, has naturally assumed the mantle of that priesthood it deposed, and perpetuated the same old heresy of Christendom under a shift of metaphor. This academic heresy has, for some time now, been to suggest that there can be any connection between perception and existence; any connection between the mind of man and the universe in which he moves; that thought has any connection with matter; that mind could in any way be other than an emergent electrochemical brain function; that any relation could exist between perceiving subject and perceived object—all of which is to say, not so much that there *is* no God, but, more effectively, that there could be no *connection* with one, even *were* there one.

Full development, for which we are genetically equipped, is pure creativity, which can only take place by thought being developed as an instrument of insight-intelligence, open to and capable of handling the awesome power of consciousness. Anything less is incomplete development which will always (no matter how much gadgetry we pile around us) cause anxiety because we aren't developing the higher levels of abstract or nonphysical thought we must have for "mental autonomy." Autonomy is the ability to create a perceptual experience not dependent on our given physical materials, even though our creative ability must arise out of those given materials.

The function of the great vaccination is to convince us that anything outside our self-generated thought and given physical world is "only imagination." Not only does this deny us a future beyond the physical, this limits present reality to the "objective"—that which is thought to be outside of and independent of us. Equally, our vaccination implies that the creative activity from insight-intelligence, should it be successful in breaking into our awareness, is an aberration, a harbinger of mental illness, leading to a collapse into chaos in our heads.

Poet Blake clearly saw this problem and opposed the lies of Newton, Locke, and The Enlightenment (wildly ironic misnomer) on which modern thought rests. Locke thought to reduce perception to an automatic reflex, rather like litmus paper, or a frog's leg twitching in the skillet. The final criterion of the real could only be found in the object of perception. Consensus on the nature of the stone was the closest we could come to "knowing what was real" while activity of the mind was relegated to the most unreal, "only imagination" in the pejorative sense of that word.

Blake, on the other hand, insisted that: "Mental things are alone real; What is called Corporeal, Nobody knows of its Dwelling Place ... Where is the Existence out of Mind or thought ... but in the Mind of a Fool?"

The Enlightenment looked on perception as a reaction by a kind of cameralike brain to impingements on it from material forces outside it. Only by being "objective" could reality be really seen, and to be objective meant to orient one's self absolutely with the deadness of the stone-out-there as the real, and strip the mind of its fuzzy subjectiveness which clouded the true picture. Today we hear psychologists and philosophers self-pityingly intoning: "Whatever reality is, we shall never know it." The real, like God, receded into the unavailable and the illusory search for the "basic building blocks of matter" began, a search for realness as the most inert possible portion of being.

Thought was considered a reflection on, or kind of photographic reviewing of, the permanent impingements on our brain by the real-out-there, impingements called "memory." Mind, at best, was the brain's reflection on its memory-impingements, which, were it truly objective, produced *reason,* a kind of abstract, nonhuman logic. Reason, though, could not logically be attributed to an emergent quality of reflecting brain and so was considered to be our "likeness to God." God became the *perfect reasoner*—the logical governor (like the governor on a machine that keeps it from spinning out of control), the mechanical computer keeping his clockwork mechanism of a stone-dead and inert universe moving in balance. Our relation to God thus shifted, in the European mind, to our capacity for "objective logic"—one gauged by a correspondence with physical matter as all there is, an alignment with the explicate order in denial of consciousness and insight, a reasoning stripped of all human elements—which meant a thought devoid of meaning, passion, love, or unity; a thought totally self-generative— the so-called "modern mind."

As a secondary result, preliterate peoples (or non-Christians or non-Europeans), devoid of academic European logic and truth tables, operating only from such human subjective traits as passion, feeling, love, joy, and so on, were considered if not devoid of godliness, at least spiritually inferior to the logical, thus godly, European mind and right subjects of exploitation (the White Man's Burden after the rape is over). It is not just coincidental that the Enlightenment view gained ascendancy as Europe moved out to enslave and plunder the world; nor that the theory of evolution should spring from what was, in effect, a scout ship for the plunderers to come; nor that the English, with their grim, methodical capacity of looting and "enormous capacity for unhappiness" should so decimate a joyful and spiritual a people as those of India.

Nearly two centuries ahead of his time, Blake knew that reality *is* perception, and a creative act, with existence and perception identical. Consciousness, existence, and perception are the primal facts of the universal process, he insisted, the perceived object the particularized result of our perceptual process. We are centers of perception and our universe radiates out from our center. Our physical body is the outward extension needed by our perceiving center for its interactions with a resulting perceptual universe.

Perception is an art to be developed, Blake claimed. The more developed a perceiver, the greater and more alive his reality. To a wise man, a visionary, an artist, or a saint, a tree is more real than it is to a fool or dullard. Every aspect of the universe is a seething caldron of possibility—when we are aligned with our "Divine

Genius" within (which is to say, when thought is aligned with in-sight-intelligence). What a thing is depends upon what our vision makes of it. We give life or deny it to our world, and must assume responsibility for every thought and act. Ordinary seeing is mechanical and dead; vision is seeing that the universe is the material for creation, not the fixed deadness of matter.

Blake lost his argument, to say the least. Indeed, there was no contest. We are now living in the pandemonium he foresaw should Newton, Locke, and company win the day, as they surely did. The "Enlightenment" proved no boon to man—just one more frying pan to switch into—and it may prove the final fire.

The priests who "stand at the narrow gate" and block man's entrance to life no longer wear vestments, but the thick-lensed spectacles of the smugly myopic, near-blind technician-bureaucrats who, because they see so darkly, deny light as a real phenomenon. Not only is our development blocked by such cultural models of despair, our true mental birth out of our physical matrix is blocked. (Do we turn on nature with such fury today because we can't get free of her?) We may be kept not just in infancy by the constrictions of a technological culture, but perhaps essentially in utero. The autistic epidemic may be but the first wave of far worse to come. We may be, after all, not so much a fallen race as an unborn one. A great imaginative energy is needed to burst us loose from this bind—an energy greater than the vast combine of isolated and arrogant thought now in control. The energy of freedom is being generated, too; out of our very need it comes, in the form of a "postulate-in-person"—lest we remain not just unborn, but go stillborn. The uterine infant can wait just so long past its delivery time, and we may be well past due.

X

Creative Imagination

The dictionary defines imagination as "the ability to create images not present to the senses." One of the first capacities to appear for development, yet perhaps the least developed, is this ability to create in a mental state images that are not present in the physical state.

Dreams are images in our heads not present to our body senses— but dreams draw *on* that physical experience. Infants may dream in one sense-idiom at a time (that is, a smell-dream, or touch-dream, etc.), and fully sensory dreaming may have to await sensory integration, which is maturational. From the beginning, we make images not present to body senses. Surely this indicates a principle thrust of development—developed or not.

Mental maturity takes place through development from concreteness, or physical experience, toward abstraction, or mental experience. All the materials from our physical, outer experience should become a source for our abstract, inner experience. Our physical life shares in a created world, and our early development is rather a copying; our developing inner life is creative, however, and can be original. Yet that inner world we create depends on both the materials and skills gained from the outer experience. This is how our life moves from the concrete to the abstract, or from the explicate order toward the implicate order from which we arise; and this is the way we develop autonomy—and survive as personalities.

When we create an internal experience out of our own store of stuff, we are perceptually self-sufficient. Perception is existence, so we can create a self-sufficient existence within our own perimeters. Since it seems that each brain has the holonomic movement within it, our perimeters are limited only by our ability. The ability to create abstract materials out of concrete experience would, if developed, allow perception to move beyond the physical—beyond body, brain, and world. This is what true autonomy is, and this is what development has for its goal.

Most dreams seem little more than "psychic flatulence," a chaos little different from our roof-brain chatter, hounding us every waking moment. Not much of this daytime "thinking" is intelligent, so why should we expect its (possible) nighttime equivalent to be any better?

Why should we assume that either dreaming or thought should appear in a developed state, rather than in a rudimentary state awaiting development? Nothing else does. As Frye says: "No one can begin to think straight unless he has a passionate desire to think and an intense joy in thinking." Surely this holds for any art or science. Creative thinking incorporates insight. Ordinary imagination may be like ordinary thinking, self-generated and sterile. Creative imagination opens to consciousness and insight.

In Dream-Time, the Australian Aborigine is one with the "Two Brothers" who eternally create the world. Here time and space are transcended and the Aborigine can draw highly specific environmental information not available to the body's five senses. Through Dream-Time he can track, without hesitation, a trail laid down a year before, though all physical signs have been obliterated.

The Uganda mother, "bonded" to her infant, knows when her infant is going to urinate and so "takes it to the bushes" ahead of time. Her brain registers that information and she acts on it. Bonding opens her to consciousness, which is the general field underlying both herself and child.

However, bodily senses are only a part of the perceptual spec-

trum available to the mind/brain. The Aborigine opens to the holonomic order when in Dream-Time and can track an ancient trail
since all time is "enfolded" in any single moment, and the trail's
original "laying-down" is unfolded through Dream-Time.

Our perception ordinarily operates through a sensory selectivity
that acts, in effect, as immunization against certain sensory possibilities. A child might see and respond to so-called extrasensory stimuli until he finds that such events upset his parents when reported,
or that his parents do not share in his experience. Then, not only
does the child not get a name-label *for* the experience (which naming lifts order out of chaos and anchors new stimuli into the conceptual system), he gets negative feedback from his principal criteria for deciding what is *real*—his parents. A "selective blindness"
toward such sensory stimuli will eventually take place. The child is
in consciousness, but his adults and their world are in thought.
When verbal thought begins, the child begins to identify with
thought and *lose* consciousness. He does this because the adult
world he *must* relate to is made of isolated thought split off from
consciousness.

John Ross describes the "editorial quality" of perceptions as
"unconscious interpretation of visual data" in which the brain *de-
cides* what it will see. Visual records are consulted before anything
is seen, so that vision is a "critical faculty capable of making deci-
sions and of rejecting information, apparently on aesthetic
grounds." The visual system may have a program, an arrangement
for perceiving shapes in time and space. "What we see is an interpretation. . . . We adopt a perceptual attitude in order to comprehend the world."[1]

We adopt perceptual attitudes as infant/children to maintain our
consensus or bond with our parents and later, society. We respond
according to an aesthetic largely ready-made, which includes heavy
doses of samskaras based on anxiety. Further, the visual system oc-
cupies the largest portion of the brain and incorporates and inte-
grates all other senses. Thus, as the visual apparatus goes, so goes
the whole sensory system and thinking itself—to the extent that we
even refer to understanding as: "I see."

Our culture sustains itself through a commonsense objectivity.

Common sense is sensory intake held to be in common with everyone, agreed upon by a majority. Poet Blake referred to the "Guinea Sun Mentality" of The Enlightenment period: " 'What,' it will be question'd, 'When the Sun rises, do you not see a round disk of fire somewhat like a Guinea?" [A British gold coin.] 'Oh no, no, I see an Innumerable company of the Heavenly Host crying, 'Holy, Holy, Holy, is the Lord God Almighty.' "

According to Blake, perception isn't something that happens to us through our senses; it is a mental act. To actively perceive, then, is to use imagination—the ability to create images not present to the senses. The more active one's imagination, the richer his perceptual experience, and the more real his world.

Blake's standard of reality was the genius—the one who could exercise his creativity to the greatest degree. The worship of God is: "Honouring his gifts in other men, each according to his genius, and loving the greatest men best: those who envy or calumniate great men hate God; for there is no other God." The genius's perception will be the most perfect since perfection means the fullest development of capacities. To the Guinea Sun Mentality in grips today, a majority vote on the sun, a consensus of so-called "normal" minds "eliminates the idiot who goes below this [norm] and the visionary who rises above it as equally irrelevant," as Frye put it.

Surely our century has seen the emergence of a "normal" as the standard of life, a norm which has become the lowest common denominator of "objectivity"—seeing *without* imagination, pretending to be a mechanical camera reporting that which is inflicted on us by what we see. We have set up our *lack* of creative vision as our model and denied the vision of the poet, saint, or genius in general.

Creativity is a function that grows out of physical development. A developed intelligence is a developed creativity, one that can interact with a manifest order or unmanifest possibility and "lift chaos into order." A passive perception can't assume responsibility for what is seen and so never sees anything outside the Guinea Sun norm. "Satan never sees," Blake observed, "he always has to be shown."

Siddha meditation often involves creative visions, perceptual activity that arises from within rather than from without. Such visions can be highly personal, instructive, revelatory; give guidance, euphoria, joy. They can be symbolic and course through a whole universe of possibility.

Ron Resch, Director of the Computer Geometry and Design Center at Boston University, attended Muktananda's Boston intensive in November of 1979. In his own words: "Following Baba's touch I saw myself from a position up over my right shoulder. My body was composed of luminescent white light. I sat cross-legged, still as a statue, suspended in the blackness of outer space. Suddenly, like a rocket taking off, a small dense shaft of white light took off from the base of my spine and roared up through the top of my head. Streaking upward, it burst open to fill the heaven with stars. After some time the white light descended again in a kind of gossamer tubular form, settling over me like dew. The lower edge of the column was intense and rippled like a plasma ring being rocked on the surface of water. The ring and column enclosed me, undulating a circle of light around where I sat.

"At the same time, a different sense became aware of my breath as 'So-Ham,' clearly related to the moving ring of light. The ring seemed to be the O of So, its movement the vibration of Ham. 'So-Ham' speeded up until they blurred together, the O of So and the MMMM of Ham merged as to sound of 'OM.' "

Ron tells about the confused skepticism that his academic mind put up over this experience, and how his academic skepticism lost out to the power and magnificence of his experience and its aftermath. He took a leave of absence to spend time with Baba and felt that his life underwent radical transformation in a short time.

A Shaktipat experience often gives us a quantum leap in perception, and the ongoing meditation experiences may be a way that the mind/brain can build up a conceptual system which can handle sensory information from a wider source than the physical world. The mental experience and the thought of a disciplined, trained mind can go beyond the limits of our ordinary world and open to larger perceptual fields. To be able to draw on or open to sources of possibility and energy beyond our concrete, physical world is one of the abilities development is designed to produce and is the way we "bond" to our next matrix.

What we are tapping into here is the area of insight, source of the postulate and revelation. Perhaps I should say we are being tapped into by this source and must learn to be so tapped. As with every thing in the holonomic movement, a dynamic interaction is what is involved. The creative source is outside our personal experience but not outside our holographic mind/brain. Experiences such as Ron Resch's very much "happen to us"; we do not, in most cases, simply fabricate them, we receive them.

There are certain subtle states in which self-generative imagination has free rein, where we can simply think of a thing and that "thing" is instantly the case for us. Roy Mason, the pharmacist, found himself in just this position. In his out-of-the-body meditation experience he found, at one point, that any image occurring to him immediately became a full-dimensional creation tangibly real right before him. These imaginative forms were not only perfectly "real" to him, they took on an independent life of their own and the situation became demonic. Roy's own creations "turned on him" and became threatening. Only through the power of the mantra, *Om Namar Shivaya*, were his unruly progeny brought to order, leaving him clear to return to his ordinary state.

Roy's experience symbolizes an actual danger in development; that we "stop-off" in some subtle realm of immature creativity, become fascinated with the possibilities and get isolated there (much as we do with ordinary confused thinking). Alignment with the holonomic order is the goal, and anything less is a delusion and snare.

Our isolated ego often stumbles into some nonordinary trickery from the subtle state, powers we can indulge in and show off. This enhances our arrogance and reduces our chance of breaking free into the Self. The value of a guide of Muktananda's stature is his absolute centeredness in the Self, and his refusal to condone sidetracks, excursions into occultism or psychic trickery. Every thought, word, and action he makes points directly to the Self, never to lesser goals, and he keeps our focus there by the force of his own person as model.

I have mentioned his daily command that we "honor the God within us," and equally his outer demand: "See God in each other." When Blake exhorts us to worship God's gifts in others and to love the greatest men best, he is right, but dangerously so. I can grant that God dwells in someone who happens to please me, whose work catches my aesthetic fancy. Less easy to grasp is that Baba means every human under every circumstance, regardless of outer appearance.

My culture loves and sponsors generalities and inoculates us against specifics. But only as I "see God in each other" moment by moment, the dirty drunk on the corner, the nasty cashier at the checkout stand, the maniac leaning on his horn or trying to side-swipe me in his rush-hour fury, the Communist and Pentagonian leaning on their mutual suicide triggers poised above us all—only then and to that extent can Baba's Truth be true for me, and my perceptual world be expanded. And the only way this is possible for me is to have experienced, within myself, an actual case of God in the other. I must have, to move from generality to the specific, a model—which is precisely what Baba is for us. We can't help, if we hang out with him long enough, but see that, indeed, God is there. And only through such real knowing can we then see this elsewhere.

Since the outer action of many people borders on madness, in their aggressive fear and paranoia, how could we "see God in them" without simple play-acting or deception? Must we accept insanity lest we be judgmental?

The issue is not what we must accept or reject, but what we do with our perception. Are we to be victimized or are we to open to creativity? Do we believe that frozen, unalterable brass-tack facts push in from out there to register digits on our helpless internal computer? Or can we accept the far greater evidence that perception is an activity, a creation of the mind/brain, that we enter into the shape of that which we see, consciously or not, that our mind encompasses far more than our conditioned brain ordinarily admits, and that we can open to that vast realm and be its instrument?

Nick Yaffe, schoolteacher from Boston, was married by Baba in his ashram at Ganeshpuri. Baba drew the couple to him for his blessing and Nick felt an enormous infusion of energy from the embrace. He returned to his place and sat down, feeling like a tree that weighed tons. The scene around him then shifted; all creation filled with blue light and the realization swept over Nick: "This is what the world really is, and always has been." He looked at Baba, who didn't seem to really be there. Baba's body was blue light and his head a luminous white light. His facial features arose and dissolved out of this white luminosity as pulsating energy.

The time came in the ceremony for the reception. Four hundred people, mostly Indians from the area, lined up to offer their blessing to the young couple and receive a customary cookie. As each came up, Nick saw that they were also his own Self, that each person also represented this unity, that they were all one.

We can't expect our mechanical eyes to furnish us with the inner truth of the other person any more than we expect our mechanical thought to create insight. Nick experienced grace, that is, insight broke through to him through Baba's power—but Nick's whole perceptual system underwent specific change as a result. Every relation, no matter how casual, has been different since, and people respond to Nick with a surprising openness and love.

We must assume responsibility for seeing and allow given patterns from the mundane world to be converted into vision, just as we must assume responsibility for our thinking and allow it to be used as an instrument of mind. We must become actors of perception, not remain the passive audience as though we are not involved. Seeing what we choose to see, we can see through the outer madness to the inner truth as Nick did. But we must desire this inner truth passionately, for passion is the link with insight. We can, through our will, when seeing the madness and chaos of a life, lift order out of that chaos, which is to see God who is the holonomic order. (Disorder is the illusion of an absence of God.)

Creative vision comes through the power of the postulate or revelation, which forms as a result of willing and shows us the bonding-power beneath the surface, the Spirit holding things together, the larger body of man of which we are both part and representative of the whole. Trained to believe that we see as a camera does—if we are "scientific and objective"—we believe that perception is separate from existence and that both happen to us as fate. The priests of social-political control, the academic bureaucrats who help dictate mass belief, must continually convince us that objectivity is the true state of affairs, that the Guinea Sun is all there is to see; and that to see God in each other and ourselves, or any such nonsense, is "only imagination" and rather beneath contempt.

And it is truly imagination, the ability to create images not present to a common sense. The power of creation is behind this ability of ours to go beyond the paltry and lift it into greatness. When caught in his own surface madness, vaccinated against his true inner state as he is, that other person can't extricate his awareness from his roof-brain chatter, paranoia, projections, and anger any more than we can for ourselves. His thought, like our thought, can only reproduce itself. *Only an outside force* can bail him out, as it can only bail us out. But in our momentary, fleeting, incidental meeting with him, in the press of the day's confusion, we can, through will, daring, and passionate longing, open up in spite of ourself, and so open him, in spite of himself, to that inner Self equally ours, that bonding-power holding things together.

An active, creative vision, open to the creative aspect of this universe, willing to be used by it, is far more powerful than the inoculated, passive receiver of automatic sensory impressions. Creative vision can lift our senses beyond the chaos of ordinary seeing and in doing this, the one we see is lifted too, whether he knows it at that moment or not.

Since we have been vaccinated against this bonding-power, we must, if we desire to know more than isolation and madness surrounding us, *willfully* move, not by verbal thought, but through passion and desire, beyond our immunization. We must, through creative and imaginative vision, dare to catch the disease of God.

XI

When Lightning Strikes

A bolt of lightning arcs the gap of earth and sky in a two-part play: energy gathers over a large terrain and collects at some vantage point—a building, tall tree, a hilltop; while a similar gathering takes place in the clouds above. When the two collections come into proximity, the earth charge leaps up, the clouds charge down, and they merge in awesome exchange.

The cloud charge is far the larger and discharges most of its energy into the earth. Some earth energy may end in the cloud, but the earth is much the richer for the encounter. (In addition, millions of tons of nitrogen are generated in this fashion each year, a principal way for renewing the earth's soil.)

As with lightning, so with genetic potential. Like attracts like. The lesser charge, built into the child, is receptive to and triggers a response from a superior or developed charge in an adult. The lesser charge is amplified in the exchange, and there is an overall renewal of nutriments for growth.

The nature of the superior force, which evokes the potential in the child, enters into the nature of the response the child makes. The awakening, the kind of development which then takes place, and the nature of the reality then experienced, are all of a part.

We have within us a potential called *Kundalini,* our personal power, which is an aspect of Shakti, the basic energy of the universe. As with any potential in us, it must be evoked by a superior stimulus of the same order. Traditionally this potential has been represented by a coiled snake (Kundalini means "coiled"). Its location is said to be at the base of the spine in the subtle body. The ancient caduceus, the two serpents coiled about a staff (adopted by the medical profession from the winged messenger, Mercury) was a representation of this energy. The Masonic Order was originally based on a discipline for unlocking this coiled power and developing it.

The techniques for awakening Kundalini range the spectrum of body/mind disciplines and are usually long and arduous. On awakening, a whole continuum of possibility unfolds that makes the effort worthwhile. No pearl could have so great a price—it's like a key to the mint. The alchemists referred to it as that which could turn lead or dross into gold. It can transform that which is common, the split anxiety-ridden social ego, into that which is rare and valuable—the whole Self.

Why, one might ask, if Kundalini is a natural potential, is it so rare and difficult? Because no natural potential can be born full-blown: the law of development holds as with walking, talking, and the most basic of functions. The possibility locked into Kundalini is our full development, not some isolated substance or ability like music or mathematics. Kundalini energy is our dormant creative energy and offers no handles for social control (or scientific analysis). It is a subtle-causal energy which, if awakened, can work for our general development of creativity and can shape within us a general guide and/or remedial process according to our need.

Within Western mythology, Kundalini awakening is represented as "stealing the fire of the gods." That the fire must be stolen, and by a hero-genius, rather than simply stimulated and developed, shows the stifling of this natural force through cultural guilt and anxiety. Our true nature is presented as forbidding and dangerous once we are split from it; as the whole person is a threat to the priests controlling a culture. If there is a "law of God," however, it is the law of development. As Frye expressed the New Testament attitude: "Those who embezzle God's talents are praised; those who are afraid to touch them are reviled."

Arousal of Kundalini twists the tiger's tail, nevertheless. The fire of the gods can burn. Discipline and control are vital to any development and critical to Kundalini unfolding because a balancing, tempering, shaping, and controlling of pure energy or power is involved. Kundalini isn't like the mastery of some particular technique or art. The only way to "master" Kundalini is to master one's total life—which is, in fact, to make one's life an instrument of Kundalini. The awakened Kundalini is the creative power itself. It is not the result of something, but that force which gives results in any undertaking.

Kundalini-Shakti may manifest in keeping with that which evokes it. Our individual power within us may mirror the outer energy bringing it forth. That's why a haphazard, unintentional awaking of Kundalini (which often happens with mail-order, do-it-yourself systems) can mean a haphazard and erratic awakened Kundalini. Don Juan, the Yaqui Indian, warned Castaneda to choose his spiritual path with care for this reason. Once unleashed, you might have a tiger by its tail.

I will never forget the afternoon, years ago, when I first read Eugene Herrigel's book, *Zen in the Art of Archery*. This is the account by a German philosophy professor of his six years under a Japanese Zen archery master in the early 1930's and his painful difficulty suspending his European logic and letting the Spirit take over and *breathe him*. At that time, for some six months I had been practicing a crude form of Zen blank-wall staring, picked up from chance reading, and sat for some two hours (of agony) daily—with nothing happening at all. I read Herrigel's beautiful little book in some three hours of total, lost absorption. On finishing, I was seized by an intense anguish of longing; I could not bear separation from *It*, the mysterious force which had finally seized Herrigel and *breathed him*.

No action offered itself to me; there was nowhere to turn to express the explosive longing within me. All I could think of was rushing up to my meditation room and sitting, once again, in front of that infernal, unproductive wall. No sooner had I done so than a huge, indescribable force *did* seize me, equally inside and outside my body and every cell. Immediately the wall disappeared, the world dropped away. All there was was this enormous force *breathing* me—the sound of my breath's great indrawing monumental and stupendous.

I was, however, incapable of dealing with It—my body panicked, knee jerk reflexed shamelessly. Instantly, the force was gone. The room was back with its infernal wall; I was again my miserable little body and puny breath. The God had come as called but—it seems I hadn't really meant it. No matter that in that second instant I regretted my first instant's reflex; the door had opened, I had refused, and it had closed. My cubic centimeter of chance had gone.

There is the admonition in the Gospels to be alert, constantly on-guard, for we never know at what instant He might come. The reason for alertness is that He generally never comes in quite the guise we expect. Or, when He comes, we are hardly prepared for the momentousness of that occasion. We want to dally a bit and discuss the issue—while the lightning bolt is instantaneous.

With Kundalini a principle of mirroring is involved. What we release on earth is released in heaven and vice versa, as the two-part cloud-earth lightning play. The nature or character of the stimulus awakening our Kundalini seems to enter into the nature or character of how that force will unfold within us, and how it will affect our life—since this is the way "God becomes many." Reading Herrigel, "It" arose to breathe me—*If I could be breathed.* Reading Muktananda years later, *It* arose again, thank God, to lead me to Muktananda, who teaches us *how to be* breathed.

Disciplines have always been around to awaken Kundalini through initiation. This works, though, only so long as a true genius-saint is there to evoke that response and nurture its growth. Kundalini-awakening doesn't institutionalize well and loses its thrust unless renewed generation by generation. The very nature of the formal elements within any discipline will produce the cultural disease of political control and constrict the process, unless a new genius of power and daring periodically sweeps the altar clean and renews the fire.

The early followers of the "way of Jesus" initiated in the simplest direct way: laying-on of hands or immersion in water whenever the need arose (as witness Philip and the Ethiopian). The results were immediate and dramatic (drunk as on new wine) and even effective in large groups (as at Pentecost when tongues of fire descended on their heads and they spoke in "tongues").

The forces of social-political control made the Gospel initiation a ritual, a union-card into the newly emerging political association eventually to seize secular control. Baptism and its ensuing "confirmation" became a method of enculturation, instilling cultural guilt and anxiety and turning the "roaring torrent of God into the broad but feeble stream of Christendom." No ritual of the church could endow one with Shakti for the church had no such power at its disposal. Political power is hardly Shakti.

When there is no power for an initiation, an earnest seeker has to try and do the work of both poles, rather as a ground charge of electricity would have to build a sufficient energy to bolt itself all the way to the cloud, unaided by any corresponding energy in that cloud. Then there is no doubling of investment of energies, as found in the superior conjunction. There may be, from an enormous self-effort, an explosive discharge, perhaps, but too often only a dissipation of personal power results.

A certain trial and error enters into any learning, but no development is designed to be by trial and error alone. The human is meant for *continual* guidance and for constant discipline and self-control. So why should meditation and spiritual practice be any different? The induction of Shaktipat and guidance of Kundalini-awakening by Muktananda is a disciplined, intelligent response to our natural need—the response life has designed and provided. Just awakening Kundalini—rare as it is—doesn't bring wholeness. It's just the kindergarten. The diploma is no more awarded on Kundalini-awakening than is a youngster ready for the concert hall after a first piano lesson.

Kundalini-awakening makes *possible* the full development which is inherent within us, but this must be the intent behind the force doing the awakening. The end is in the beginning—the goal is inherent within the nature of the awakening. Some people bristle at the claim that on being given the touch by Muktananda, one experiences the actual goal, the inner Self, God as our own Being, but that is the actual fact. Part of our religious vaccination *against* God is convincing us that suffering, privation, and random-chance hardship are the marks of a spiritual journey. But nothing *else* in development is designed to be suffering or random chance, so why should spiritual development? As I made clear in *Magical Child,* development is meant to be a joyous, magnificent venture.

A child would do poorly, indeed, if we tried to teach him to play the piano with a silent keyboard, saying, in effect, that he is not supposed (or not fit) to hear what it is all about until he has achieved perfection. In the same way, our spiritual growth is poor when we have no notion what the goal is about. The Guru principle is designed to give this actual experience as the *starting point*— which makes eminently good sense. The Guru principle is designed not only to awaken our power and furnish a model for its development, he is also designed to *lend us his power,* precisely as a parent lends the child his power, both to give a clear demonstration of what development will give us and to get that development under way. Herrigel tells how the Zen master would use the student's bow and so lend that bow his power, after which, for a time, the bow would respond equally for the student and let him know what to look for.

We learn from the concrete *to* the abstract, from the specific application to the broad application. The radical discontinuity between our spiritual goal and our ordinary locked-up perceptions is bridged through an initial grace. Having that bolt of lightning meet us (always *more* than halfway) gives us the vision to see where we are going. Knowing where we are going, and with light to see by, it's a happy journey.

The Guru is a function which leads us from the darkness of ignorance into the light of knowledge. Knowledge in this case is not verbal information, but perceptual experience. Muktananda penetrates our ignorance with a burst of light itself, not vague descriptions.

David Nowe, of New York City, received the touch at an intensive. An orange flame started at the space between his eyebrows, swirled as an expanding energy of warmth throughout his body, out beyond him until it encompassed him in an egg-shaped cocoon of pure love. He remained in this ecstatic space for some ten minutes, his body automatically doing the yogic bastrika breathing (of which David had no previous knowledge). For months afterward, the process repeated each time he sat for meditation.

This is a Shakti experience which has no correlates in ordinary life and is magnificent to its recipient. Not that an egg-shaped cocoon of orange flame is the full nature of God or state of the Self; but magnificence, love, and joy *are* that state, which can be expressed in an infinite number of ways. An experience of this gets spiritual practice going, serves as an ever-present model for development, and makes practice worthwhile.

Within the larger body of man the Guru principle is the continual "postulate arriving full-blown in the brain." He comes in response to a prolonged and passionate quest for wholeness. He is the Spirit expressed as the Son which leads to the Father; the strength through wholeness which unifies the orders of energy. As Teilhard said, there is no being except in a mode of being. To be in this world is to be born into this world. For the Guru to function here, it must be born into and expressed in this world generation by generation.

Somehow this happens in India, as it so miserably failed to happen in Christendom. Jesus was convinced that He, the Guru principle, would "come again" within the generation. If the Guru principle came, it did so esoterically—in secret. Publicly we got popes, bishops, and plagues of priests. As Blake said: "Genius dies with its possessore & comes not again till Another is Born with it."

My years of church-going were like going to the tomb of a dead saint. Pilgrimage can be a great spiritual exercise. Just as there are "power spots" perpetuated by the American Indians, there can be power at the shrines of great saints. But spiritual awakening, guidance, discipline, and growth can't take place through shrines. You couldn't teach children music by taking them to the tomb of Beethoven once a week.

The Gospels of Jesus claimed that you can make any kind of breach except that against the Holy Spirit,[1] the power that unites— for you then isolate yourself into the narrow confines of your self-generating thought. The Guru Gita states the same thing: deny the

Guru and you deny that you have any connection with power and insight. If we deny that wholeness, or perfection, is possible to an actual Guru-person *here and now,* we deny that wholeness or perfection can be other than a vague abstract idea or mythical notion. This effectively rules the possibility of wholeness out of our awareness or acceptance.

On the other hand, we are trained to grasp things—to reach out and clutch, seize, bend, manipulate, dominate. The function of wholeness can't be grasped, we must be grasped by it. The weak explicate order can't grasp the power of the holonomic system. To say that Jesus wasn't the Holy Spirit, that the Holy Spirit was Jesus, is not a cute play on words. Muktananda isn't the Guru. The Guru is Muktananda because he lets himself be so grasped. This can only be done by developing one's self to the fullest in order to be capable of *being* grasped. Only power can handle power—to him who has it *can* be given, just as "Only he who obeys can command" (as Baba reminds us). A weak, flaccid piety is an instrument only for a weak, flaccid piety. An instrument for dispensing the fire of the gods must be a fiery instrument.

Lightning strikes when the cloud accumulation comes into proximity with a primed ground one. My friend, Mac Gudgeon, a television director from Melbourne, Australia, saw Muktananda's photograph among others in a montage on a record jacket. Baba was unknown to Mac, but all else faded, Baba's picture leapt out of context and took over; Mac fell into an infinite space within his Self, filled with peace and power, and remained there for some two hours. Everything in his life changed rapidly from that point and he was led to meet Muktananda (and, with his wife and child, has been with Baba since).

We were all primed with Shakti at birth, but our enculturation erodes our power and we must often rebuild a sufficient charge to attract more. With Patricia Kuboske, a social worker from South Bend, Indiana, that accumulation was rapid and progressive. In 1973, she went to visit an old high school friend, concerning some material for her graduate studies. She found that her friend was in Ganeshpuri, India, at Muktananda's ashram. Intrigued, Patricia wrote and received from her friend various books about Muktananda and was regularly sent a newsletter from the ashram. One day, as she opened a newsletter just received, out from the print emerged " ... an egg-shaped, plasmalike moving blob of transparent energy," growing in volume and suddenly enveloping everything. Startled, Patricia threw off the strange experience, but the power of it was too much to ignore. Determined to go to India herself, she got a job as a house painter to raise some quick cash for the trip. She fell, however, seriously injuring her ankle. That night, Muktananda came to her in a dreamlike vision, touched her ankle; the next morning it was healed. She returned to work that day and was in India shortly thereafter (and has been with Baba since).

Muktananda is able to reach out and literally inject insight directly into a person's brain and life, and then guide the ensuing development, the reordering of that brain into creative coherence. This is possible only because the capacity is also within that other brain. Spark triggers spark, but the size of the one doing the responding to our small and feeble efforts is beyond our calculation.

Surely this Shaktipat effect is unique in history—so was Jesus. But surely the critical nature of our current history is equally unique. Extremes of crisis call for extremes of response. The passionate question of a mass driven to the brink of chaos triggers its response. We ask and we receive. We knock and the door opens to us. Whether we enter or not is up to us. This is a door, however, that doesn't hang around open, waiting for us to debate the issue.

XII

Meeting of Minds

Once a curiosity-seeker came up to Baba in *darshan,*[1] daily meeting, and asked imperiously: "Can you read my mind?" "What would I want to wander around in your confusion for?" Baba retorted.

Baba *can* wander in our confusion, if needed, though he picks his way with care. For instance, after my first week with him, I had to go home and put my affairs in order so that I could come back and stay. I wanted to ask him, in my last evening darshan, to bless my "reminder" (a metal trinket I wear around my neck as a reminder not to lose myself in the world). Blessing means bestowal of power, so I didn't treat the request lightly, but rehearsed it carefully.

In line for darshan, however, a feeling of abject unworthiness swept me. In spite of my rehearsal, my nerve failed me and I could not ask for anything. Instead, I hunkered down, ducked, bowed rapidly, and tried to get away unnoticed. Even faster, though, Baba reached out, caught my reminder cord, hauled me before him, took off my reminder, handled it, chatted a bit, rehung it around my neck, and waved me on, laughing.

The episode took no more than ten or fifteen seconds and was but one of hundreds of incidents each evening in darshan. This cemented our relationship, though, for, among many things, I knew then that he saw through my silliness into my true needs and responded according to need, not silliness. His constant reminder-claim is that he sees us as perfect, the Self he chooses to see, and which he daily challenges us to see also, in our self and each other.

Was Baba "reading my mind"? Hardly. My mind, or thought, was full of garbage, but my heart was full of longing and our heart, Baba claims, is where our true Self dwells. But how, you might insist, did he know, unless he is mind-reading? Well, what would we have explained if we used the term *mind-reading*? Almost nothing. Obviously, one person doesn't "read" another's mind or thoughts, and mine was chaos anyway. To say he read my heart would be more accurate, but not much of an answer.

Consider Francesco Sastre, a student from Barcelona, Spain, traveling in Southern India in 1976, looking for a particular Buddhist school and ending, by "accident," at Muktananda's ashram in Ganeshpuri. Baba was in America at the time, and the focus of the ashram is Nityananda, Baba's Guru, whose statue is a principal point of attraction. Francesco joined the chanting, which seemed the main occupation at the ashram, but had such peculiar rushes of heat and energy over his body, and strange visions and impressions that he started to leave. Someone urged him first to go meditate in the Cave (a large underground meditation room), and he did. There he had a vision of Nityananda, whose picture and statue he had seen. That familiar image then became Muktananda, whose picture Francesco had not seen, and who was a complete stranger to him. In Sastre's vision, Baba said to him, "Relax, your Kundalini is awakening. I will take care of you until you are perfect." Then this image of Baba merged right into Francesco's body.

Francesco stayed at the ashram for several months, with increasing meditation experiences, feelings of peace and harmony, and an exceptional outburst of creative writing. He returned to Spain, heard that Baba was going to be in Paris, and traveled there to see him. He was apprehensive about this formal meeting, but it took place by chance, most informally, in a garden where Baba was walking. Baba called him over to him and asked: "We have met in Ganeshpuri, haven't we?"

Dr. D. K. Salunkhe, nutritionist of the Food Science Department, Utah State University, was in Istanbul, Turkey, as a consultant to a university there, setting up a department of nutrition. The doctor returned to his hotel room at midnight one evening, took two sleeping pills, and went to bed. He was awakened at three A.M. by a voice commanding: "Get dressed quickly and leave this hotel." The doctor ignored the intrusion, but the voice grew louder and finally imperious in its demand. Disturbed, the doctor got up, dressed, and stumbled down and out to the sidewalk. Immediately after he was outside, a huge earthquake hit, leveling the hotel.

On his return home, Salunkhe confided this episode to his sister. Now his sister had met and become a follower of Muktananda's (the connecting link always must be there), and insisted her brother go see Baba. He undertook the journey and as he came up in darshan line for that first meeting, Baba's face lit up in recognition and he asked, an impish grin on his face: "So how was that visit to Istanbul?"

Cameron Wilson, biologist at Thomas Jefferson College, had taken a leave of absence to remain in Oakland and "be with Baba." He lived some distance from the ashram, but went there daily. One day at home, he was flossing his teeth before going out on a busy round of activities. Suddenly he felt extremely heavy and had an overwhelming urge to sit down and sink into meditation. His full schedule pressed him, though, and with real effort he fought off the compulsion and steadily held to that tooth-flossing.

That evening at the ashram, Baba's talk was about meditation. "I'm always trying to get people to meditate," he said. "Just this afternoon I was trying to get a man to meditate, but all he wanted to do was floss his teeth." He then looked at Wilson and went through a pantomime flossing-motion, with a big grin on his face.

Such a magnificent "analogic function" is involved here that I hesitate giving my petty little digital "explanation"—but such is my fate. Consider that all time and space are "enfolded" within the implicate order. The implicate order is consciousness. The Guru-principle *is* that consciousness, the Guru-person open to and one with that order of energy. But since "everything" is enfolded in the implicate order, to open to it would be, in effect, to open to a chaotic flood of instantaneous impression. I have known so-called "psychics," for instance, who were good enough at some kind of brain-picking to impress the ignorant and gullible. They seem to open to the implicate order, but in a very haphazard fashion which floods them with a sea of impressions from which they must randomly pick items. Some items may fit the listeners and if a listener makes quick enough response, the psychic can narrow the flood down to a few vague generalities that may have some correspondence. (Even so famous a psychic as Peter Hurkos reportedly has only about a 30-percent relevancy in his impressions.)

This is largely garbage-wading and remotely different from the so-called "siddhis" of the developed Yogi. Baba is surely never subject to a "flood of impressions." What lifts order out of the inherent chaos is his function as Guru, which means his relation to his student. Truth is any phenomenon in alignment with the holonomic order and the only thing real to a person in truth is "the truth." So the only information that is "real" and so registered with Baba is that of his relationship, or alignment, with a student. That is what is available to Baba, as available as his own thought—and, indeed, no different to him. ("From whom no secrets are hid, no desires unknown," as the Book of Common Prayer expressed it, can be unnerving in actuality.)

Anything leading toward alignment of the holonomic order is true; anything leading away from it is false. Francesco's "vision" of Baba in the cave would be dismissed by Western psychology as "subjective hallucination"—as would my original experience of being tossed like a ping-pong ball from one end of the universe to the other. But these were the *truest and most real moments* of our lives—perhaps the first absolute truth and reality we had experienced *since encompassing more of the holonomic order than our usual surface isolations.*

Teacher-student relating is the issue with Baba, nothing else is relevant. When a mathematician passionately pursues a mathematical possibility for years, he does not get, as answer, a musical sonata or architectural insight into bridge-building. The Guru functions as Guru—big enough job, that.

This is the reason for Baba's absolute clarity, and why he is the most "totally present" human I have ever encountered. Each instant offers him that which is related to that instant, as does each person. Extraneous material flooding into the moment confuses, clouds the issue, and blocks the flow of actual and real relatedness, or reality, enfolded in each instant. A "flood of impressions" is the work of a rank amateur, not a master. So "mind-reading" seriously misses the point, which point is to be in the instant moment's unfolding, since this is the way the holonomic order functions as a unit and maintains wholeness. We are almost never in the moment—we are always reflecting, anticipating, prestructuring, attempting to predict and control in our anxiety and isolation. All of which isolates us ever further into self-generated surface-level thinking which can only reproduce itself.

Voluntary acts are essential to development and learning. Muktananda seems never to impinge upon anyone, or overtly bring about some nonordinary condition, not even healing. Around him, however, conditions continually unfold so that if we are receptive, change, healing, assistance, and so on are forthcoming. We must enter into "the Act of the Word," though, we must, in fact, take the outward initiative. Then we find the inward conditions ready—we are met more than halfway once we move toward wholeness. If we go to Muktananda for healing, he instructs us to *meditate.* He throws the ball right back to us. He uses our disease as a means of forcing us to focus our fragmented will, pull our disjointed thought together. Will is our power to act, and the extent of the Guru's power in our life is the extent of our willingness to open to that power.

A young woman with advanced leukemia and supposedly only a month or so left to live came; Baba embraced her, stroked her forehead, and told her to go home and meditate that she would be well. She did and some three weeks later was completely free of this dread blood cancer, to the astonishment of her doctors.

Jacque Anderson, of Mercer Island, Washington, mother of two, suffered a severe case of ulcerated colitis. She had spent several thousand dollars on treatment, including Rolfing and psychiatry. She met Baba, told him of her plight. He poked her in three places between the eyes; she felt his fingernails must have pricked her; he told her to go and repeat the mantra in the meditation hall. She did.

Severe vibrations began, shaking her colon, and bastrika breathing began. This continued, unabated, for over an hour, and then stopped. She has never had a trace of trouble in the five years since.

Earlier I mentioned the Shaktipat experience of David Nowe. A twenty-four-year-old New Yorker, David was completely crippled with rheumatoid arthritis. His joints were grossly enlarged, he had to wear special cloth shoes, walked with a cane, and was under heavy sedation. He had undergone every known treatment, to no avail. Following Shaktipat, his condition improved steadily. Finally, during an intensive with Baba in Oakland a couple of months later, he locked into the lotus position (which would have been impossible ordinarily), bastrika breathing began, and he strarted doing (without volition) huge frog-leaps off the floor without breaking lotus. Those around him reported his body moving eighteen to twenty inches off the floor; huge cracking noises were heard. The violent movements continued for a couple of hours, and he emerged from the experience cured, his limbs and joints normal. He had no relapse and has been with Baba since.

The connections with Baba can be even more tenuous. Dianne Johnson, a student at Mills College at the time, had met Baba in 1970 with no relationship established. She did not meditate, do the mantra, or think of him afterward. Yet when he returned in 1974, she visited him again, with again no response. The morning of January 10, 1975, she awoke with a headache too intense to ignore. She had had her usual physical checkup only two weeks earlier and was, apparently, in splendid health—but found herself being rushed to an emergency ward, and was shortly in the intensive-care unit. A great amount of blood was found in her spinal cord; a team of doctors, neurosurgeons, and so on were called in. Two hours later, she heard that the diagnosis was massive cerebral hemorrhage. She knew, of course, what that meant, that her chances of survival were slim.

Suddenly, in a burst of brilliant blue light, she clearly perceived Muktananda, whom she had not thought of, and was surprised to see. Her vision clearly "told her" that she would be healed completely; that Baba was her Guru, her true, inner Self; that she would spend her life with him. Exhaustive tests and explorations were made in the days that followed, but no trace of damage could be found. Unable to comprehend the findings, the doctors finally concluded that she had "blown a blood vessel" and had undergone a spontaneous healing. Out of the hospital, Dianne sold her belongings and went with Muktananda—and has been with him since.

The ways in which the Guru-principle functions are unfathomable. Ellen Gillanders tells of a young man dying of a brain tumor. Total paralysis had set in and no communications seemed to be there. The young man showed all the signs of acute anxiety, though, his muscles rigid, his breath shallow; open-eyed, he stared fixedly, with a terrible urgency, at the ceiling. Nurse Gillanders, a Baba devotee, brought in a little tape machine and played, over and over through the night, Baba's singing of the mantra, *Om Namah Shivaya* (I bow to Shiva, the God within).

The next morning, her patient was relaxed, his breathing gentle, his eyes closed. When he opened them, they were lucid and calm. The family gathered and he died in apparent peace. At the moment of his death, the unique and peculiar Indian scent which Baba puts on the peacock feathers carried during an intensive (and indelibly etched into all our nostrils) flooded the room. Everyone in the room exclaimed over the sudden wafting of such a strange and pungent smell. People passing in the hall stopped to inquire about the scent coming out of the room so strongly, and Nurse Gillanders was, of course, filled with awe, wonder, and gratitude.

I recall how intrigued I was, years ago, with Carl Jung's forays into "synchronicity," a pseudoscientific attempt to explain nonordinary phenomena and the way thinking at times seemed to influence reality (so vigorously denied by academic thought). How pallid his examples and explanations seem after time around Baba. Late in January of 1980, young David Maxey from Victoria, Canada, wintering with Baba at Miami Beach, ran out of money and needed to return home. Walking with a friend, he told him of his plight. His friend replied that work was available on a roof-construction job nearby (and construction was David's line of work) *if* David had some tin snips. David had neither snips nor money, and laughingly told his friend of an account he had just read by a Sufi saint saying that if need arose, one should go down to the ocean and pray, and a fish would appear and fill the need. (There is a similar story in the Gospels of Jesus.)

They were, at that moment, walking over the broad bridge that spans Indian Creek, a large saltwater canal running through Miami Beach. They noticed a school of fish churning the water at the canal's (cement-lined) edge (a rare occasion, I might add). Impulsively, they hopped the fence and ran to the water's edge; the fish scattered, and there in about five feet of water, they clearly saw a boxed pair of tin snips. In mounting excitement, David remarked that if they had a board with a nail in the end, they might hook the box. Not five feet away, against the otherwise clean bank, was just such a board, a large nail hooked in its end. They snagged the box and brought it up. It was brand-new, could not have been in the water very long, the price tag, $14.95, intact. David brought it to me in a state of near-giddy excitement, saying he knew that all would be well with him no matter where he went, that the Guru was with him.

Baba uses nonordinary capacities only in the most practical way. John Ebling, civil engineer from Oregon, is now Baba's audio technician. He handles the extensive equipment for recording, broadcasting, hall amplification, and so on during programs. He sits alongside the wall to the immediate left of Baba's chair, for he must watch for continual clues from Baba concerning employment of the equipment. In February of 1980, a movie-actress devotee of Baba's married Japan's top-rated popular singer. A mass of television people and newsmen swarmed the meditation hall where Baba performed the ceremony. Baba's marriage ceremony called for a switch of tapes from a particular Vedic chant to flute music. While the switch generally takes place at about the same time at each wedding, Baba demands absolute precision for the moment and always gives a visual cue to his sound men.

This time, though, the enormous block of cameramen and reporters pushed beyond their boundaries and crowded between Ebling and Baba. Ebling stood up to try to see Baba, but was completely closed off. Just as he was about to panic, he was startled to see a perfect hole, like a porthole in a boat, open up through the bodies in front of him, and there he clearly saw Baba who turned to him, grinned, and pantomimed flute-playing. He quickly reached down and threw the appropriate switches as hall monitors were struggling to get through the mass of reporters to tell him to switch the music. (People on the other side of Baba saw him suddenly turn to the large body of newsmen, grin, and make flute-motions, swing around, and continue the ceremony.)

In his ordinary state, a Guru is open to the implicate and insight realms, and through him alignment flows into our more restricted world. But he is more than just a channel. He shifts back and forth. Sometimes he withdraws; in effect, he isn't quite here. Miguel Serrano spoke of a long series of meetings with Anandamayi Ma. Sitting with hundreds of others, he watched this remarkable and very old saint. One day she would seem to him incredibly young, vivacious, almost coquettish and flirtatious; at other times, ancient. Occasionally, he caught a glimpse of her that sent a chill up his spine—he sensed something to her that was no longer human. She had really gone beyond all the physical orders of being and just kind of drifted back in among her followers as the occasion demanded. All of us around Muktananda for any length of time pick up a similar sensing, that which borders on the uncanny and the unknown and which stands as a bit of tantalizing qualification, lest my neat map-making here presume to be the actual terrain.

XIII

Mantra

No Eastern practice aroused my Western skepticism so strongly as the theory of mantra. The notion that certain words had power and could affect our mind/brain and even our relation to the world smacked of mumbo jumbo to the extreme, bordering on magic incantation. I could see how repeating some phrase harnesses roof-brain chatter and links it with a kind of autosuggestion. Salesmen keep slogans on their mirrors, dashboards of their car, and so on, affirming: "I am confident, buoyant, happy, and irresistible. I will sell a million dollars worth today." Their "mantra" seems to promote a positive stance; they tend to become the slogan they behold.

Sounds, vibrations, electromagnetic fields, can influence the brain. My friend Robert Monroe has developed binaural beats of varying types which, heard through earphones, affect brain-wave coherence. He calls the effect "hemi-sync"—for hemispheric synchronization. I have watched wave-tracings as a "trainee" relaxes and listens to one of Bob's gateway tapes. Synchronization takes place within a few minutes, a single slow pulse takes over, and a different perceptual ballgame often opens at that point.

Bob suspects that earphones have some influence on the brain because of the magnetic field they set up. For instance, his own extraordinary out-of-body experiences, which lasted for years, followed an attempt to perfect a sleep-learning device. He was his own subject and for months slept with earphones attached, trying various ways to teach the sleeping brain. His efforts were futile (the brain doesn't seem to learn that way), but he had, after that, the unexpected phenomenon of spontaneous out-of-body experiences; he slipped from the physical to subtle state at the slightest relaxation, and generally in spite of himself.

When we look at the brain from the holonomic model, Monroe's experience and the theory of mantra make more sense. We know the brain operates through electrochemical actions, but wave-vibrations are at the base of even that activity. Since the brain constructs its world-view by an interweaving and relating of energy vibrations, any vibration must have some kind of effect, and some more than others.

For several decades the French physician, Alfred Tomatis, has studied, at his research institute, the effects of sound on us humans.[1] Tomatis considers the hearing-listening mechanism the "primary organ of our emerging consciousness." He has been particularly interested in the effect of chanting on the body: why, for instance, Benedictine monks need only three hours sleep a night so long as they chant six to eight hours a day. Gregorian chant, like Eastern chant, springs from sources that were ancient before the Christian Era. Over thousands of years, Tomatis asserts, man developed a form of vocalization which had maximum benefits for the mind and body.

Tomatis speaks of "discharge sounds," which tend to fatigue, and "charge sounds," which give tone, health, and peace of mind. Sound proves one of the major sources of brain stimulus by which dynamic mental vitality is maintained. Vocal sounds directly resonate through the skull, chest, and body. Our personally produced resonances can charge and revitalize our body and brain. Tomatis points out that the ear is our instrument of balance, but he refers to far more than just our alignment with the Earth and gravity. Balance means the tonus of the body; it means gestures, the nonverbal language of the whole environment, the spatial dynamic "on top of which we can superimpose vision." Tomatis considers the skin a "piece of differentiated ear" and the whole body, its joints, muscles, spine, bones—everything used to maintain balance in gravity—is tied to the vestibular labyrinth that keeps all in balance.

Most chants come within the band width for charging the brain, according to Tomatis. Further, in order to follow the tradition underlying all chants, one's breathing must slow enormously, and a marked control of sound production be developed in order to sustain the long, slow-paced rhythms. This "slowest possible breathing is a sort of respiratory yoga . . . the subject must be in a state of absolute tranquillity in order to do it."

Mantra repetition, as practiced in Siddha meditation, uses both this vocal-change form and an inner, silent form that maintains, in effect, the outer vocal form. Either way, it is a form of singing and, for some reason, produces euphoria, calms the system, and brings coherence in place of discord.

Many of the Earth's creatures sing in some fashion. I have always loved Carpenter's account of the large gibbons of Thailand who, as a group, climb to the treetop every daybreak and sing, in unison, a clearly marked octave-scale tune. At sunrise, the climax of the morning chant is reached, the gibbons "trill" on their highest note, their bodies go into ecstatic quivering, and then they subside into a profound peace and quiet.[2]

The "songs" of the humpback whales are astonishing in scope and richness and remind me of antiphonal chant. Research into the great-brained creatures of the sea show that they live in a world of sounds. We tend to interpret other creature's sounds as forms of economic communication, territorial declaratives, and so on, which may be shortsighted of us. Most animal sounds are probably forms of singing and ecstatic gestures. If the song serves other functions, that may be part of nature's economy.

In the creation theories of Shaivism, sound is the first expression of reality-formation. Sound appears as an explosive burst, with matter and light secondary aspects. That primordial sound is eternally present in the creation, according to Shaivism, since the creation is sustained by that sound. This creation takes place for each of us as our own brain develops, and we can replicate the creation through its sound, the mantra *Om* (oh-mm). That is, yogic theory says *Om* is the first creative sound itself, and the sustaining sound of creation. When we make the sound, our sound and that primal sound cohere, resonate—which is to say, we become one with that basic creative power since both sound and its creation are "enfolded" within our mind/brain. To say that we can "unfold" power through sound is thus not quite so illogical.

I didn't care for the recent "big-bang" theory of creation the cosmologists came up with. I much preferred Fred Hoyle's more elegant steady-state theory, but my aesthetics seemed to be outweighted. The big-bang group claims that there is a basic vibration in the universe, a constant background sound picked up on all the radio telescopes, which they believe is the sound of the initial universal explosion itself, still reverberating throughout the cosmos. So on this one point our hypothesizing cosmologists and those ancient Yogi explorers of the inner world have a common ground.

Yogic philosophy states that if we explore deeply enough the vast inner depths of mind we arrive at the outermost reaches of space. The outer is contained within the inner, rather than the commonsense appearance to the contrary. If we go through the "four bodies" (already mentioned), each correspondingly smaller, we will reach the heart of creation, the bindu or blue pearl, a point of reference, rather than place or thing, from which all creation radiates out.

So the thrust of Siddha practice is to get to that central point in the most direct way, immediately within one's own mind/brain. From that point the whole outer universe is available for the same direct, personal interaction (which is not quite the case with radio telescopes or space probes). One way for arriving at this central point within is through the mantra. When we repeat the primordial sound, we link our brain with the consciousness and insight of the creation itself, and bring our mind/brain into resonance with the whole.

The sound *Om* gives rise to the sound *Hamsa*. *Ham* is considered by yogic tradition the sound the life-force makes when entering us on our inbreath; *sa* is the sound it makes on the outbreath. Where they merge they form the primal sound *Om*. This takes place all the time, at every breath, according to yogic theory. All we need do is become aware of it by practicing it consciously. Our outer attention will finally merge with the inner mechanism. When resonance finally occurs we sense the creative first-sound at each breath and move into alignment with the universal process; we become aware of our unity with God. Each breath is then recognized as *in*spiration in its original sense, breathing in the Spirit.

The Sanskrit meaning for *Hamsa,* "I am That," or "I am God," makes sense within this understanding, and we see that the sound the radio telescopes pick up, that constant background vibration heard from the cosmos, is, according to Eastern tradition, the very word: "I am God." (And I, for one, think that's neat.)

The practice of Hamsa meditation is coupled with *Hamsa japa*—the constant inner repetition of the word. We try (and it takes real effort and will) to remember to say *Ham* on every inbreath and *sa* on the outbreath throughout the day, regardless of what we are doing. That is, we try to carry over our meditation into every second of our mundane worldly life. Finally, we become aware of *ham* and *sa* even while talking aloud, reading, figuring, working, or whatever. The result is alertness (we are in tune with everything), tranquility (we are at unity with everything), and centeredness (all is enfolded within our own particular little skull and heart so we don't need a criterion based on outside sources, we aren't pulled off-center into eccentricity).

You might assume that just any phrase would work, but this is not the case. A true mantra is "charged," alive, because it has been handed down for centuries, and it has been handed down because it *is* alive. A certain "archetypal" energy might result from ages of use: the passion, intensity, and will of millennia of Yogis might in itself create a subtle energy connected with the mantra. Perhaps all that subtle power gets enfolded in the name and unfolds for us in our practice. At any rate, true mantras are of consciousness, not of surface thought and semantic fabrications. A supposed private, individual mantra, made for each of us, can only contribute to our self-generative and isolated ego position, which is hardly what the Siddhas had in mind. Part of the power of the Siddha lineage is through the mantra, which is passed from Guru to Guru and so remains charged and alive. When we repeat such a mantra, we evoke the investment of that lineage from its holonomic enfolding.

Om Namah Shivaya is another variation of the primordial sound. It means "I bow to Shiva," the God within my heart. Not only does this resonate with the primordial power, it establishes our alignment; we acknowledge the hierarchy of mind/brain; we acknowledge that our surface-level ego and its verbal thought is an instrument of that primordial principle. This involves a certain surrender of ordinary enculturated ego-dominance, but brings about the harmony of alignment, in place of isolation and anxiety. Such alignment takes time to unfold fully because resonance with the primordial principle means resonance with the universal creative power. It takes power to handle or synchronize with power, and power is developmental like everything else.

The mantra is universal, not sectarian. I close my lectures and workshops with five minutes of *Om Namah Shivaya* chanting followed by a five-minute silent meditation on it. Conservative "Calvinist" audiences, Roman Catholics, urban-sophisticate agnostics, all are moved by the mantra. Recently I received a letter from a dentist who heard me speak at a college. He followed my arguments on childbirth, rearing, development, and so on, well enough, but resented ten minutes spent with mantra-repetition. He was convinced it stultified the mind, though he found that mantra occupying his mind during his long drive home that night.

He knew I was giving another lecture the next evening, some fifty miles from where I gave the first. He made out a list of questions for me, which were, actually, calling me to task for my fall from logical grace. He intended confronting me with this list after my lecture. He followed the arguments even better the second time, so, rather diffidently, went ahead with the mantra at the end. Immediately when the mantra began, he felt a great weight pressing down on his head and shoulders. This lasted throughout the five minutes of singing. When the lights dimmed and silent meditation on the mantra began, that great weight suddenly lifted and he floated free into a space or state of awareness he had never experienced before. (He found himself, of course, in the state of meditation.) When he came out of the meditation he quietly left the hall. His list of questions seemed pointless. Something had happened that was beyond all argument. The mantra had carried him into resonance, and things were changed.

Most mantra stories (and they are legion) are improbable to uninitiated ears. A meditator from New York City tells of an obscene phone call she received one day. She picked up the receiver, said hello, and was caught off-guard by a barrage of obscenities. She was stunned but heard herself say: *Om Namah Shivaya.* The voice at the other end stopped; a moment's silence ensued, then the caller said, "What was that, lady?" She repeated the mantra. "Say that again," the voice demanded. She obliged and the caller hung up. An hour later the phone rang again: "Lady," the same man asked, "What were those words again?" She told him, he thanked her, and hung up. The next day he called again and asked: "Lady, where did you get those words? They've been going over and over in my head ever since, and I've never felt so great in my life!"

Since the power of the mantra is said to be the actual power of the creative process itself, and our brain is a hologram of the larger hologram, the coherence of mind/brain and body which mantra brings can extend to the physical world itself. Princeton University (and Siddha) student Mark Kennedy was camping in Hawaii with a friend. They found a particularly beautiful beach between two mountain ridges jutting out like an open V into the sea. The beach was deserted and inviting. They didn't know it was deserted because the configuration of high mountains formed, in storms, a vortex effect that created monstrously destructive winds and waves at that spot. They pitched their tent far out on the sands, near the surf. In the middle of the night, the grandfather of all storms broke, the roar deafening. They sat up and began chanting the mantra, *Om Namah Shivaya.* (There wasn't much else to do.) The winds were tremendous and they heard waves crashing on all sides, but their tent held, somehow. The storm subsided at dawn and they crawled out to survey their situation. The waves had obliterated the beach all around them, leaving intact about a thirty-foot island of sand, in the middle of which sat their intact tent. The water subsided and they left the area.

Ron Friedland is a corporation lawyer from Chicago and Muktananda's "right-hand man" in America. (He is president of Siddha Yoga Foundation in this country.) While Baba was in Miami Beach, Ron, an avid pilot, ordered a new twin-engine craft supposedly of the finest engineering. With his mother, he was going to fly by commercial transport down to San Juan, Puerto Rico, pick up the new plane, and fly it to Miami. Muktananda urged Ron to let some pilot bring the plane up; Ron insisted that he had the plane thoroughly researched, it was tops in its field, absolutely safe, and he wanted very much to fly it himself. Baba insisted he didn't like that particular plane, but finally said "All right, but don't forget the mantra."

Three hundred and sixty miles out of San Juan, over the Atlantic, Ron approached cruising altitude, felt a thump, looked out and saw that his right wing had crimped, its shape distorted, the aluminum skin popping, as the right motor sputtered and died. The plane, with its crippled wing and dead engine, spun out of control. Ron began a serious battle to right the craft, his mother began a serious mantra repetition. Ron brought the plane into some semblance of balance, opted for a return to San Juan, and managed the course reversal, battling his controls each instant to stay aloft. He joined the mantra and began to prime the dead engine in hopes of getting it started. Suddenly it roared to life and immediately the plane was more manageable. They flew the three hundred and sixty miles back and landed, at which point the right engine quit again.

The mechanic was puzzled. The pressure-relief valve, which compensates for the difference of gas-tank pressure at high altitudes, had failed. The wing tank had exploded, thrown gasoline everywhere, all over the right engine and wing. By all rights, the plane should have burst into flame. Further, loss of the gas, and the general damage, made operation of that right engine improbable, to say nothing of flying with so seriously crippled a wing. Yet they had flown in with both engines operating. On every count, he said, Ron shouldn't be there. The plane shouldn't have flown, the engine shouldn't have run; they should have gone down in flames.

For myself, repetition of *Om Namah Shivaya* gives calmness in crisis, a peculiar conviction that all is well in spite of outward appearance, and an alert euphoria. Coming back from a seminar recently, our 727 hit the grandaddy of thunderstorms, the giant plane tossed like a leaf, our bellies pitched from ceiling to floor, people tossed their cookies, children cried, the man opposite me had a noisy heart attack followed by stroke and paralysis (they had to stretcher him off later).

Ordinarily my heart would have leaped to my throat and I would have joined my neighbor in a coronary. Instead, the mantra leaped up from my heart, singing. I went with the mantra and found myself simply processing information. An alert responsiveness swept me; every facet of the scene around me was noted in a neutral state free of fear. Not that I felt safe; "safe" indicates outcome, something of the future injected into the scene. I was processing present information only, without the distortion of imaginings about a future that didn't exist.

This is not to suggest that we employ the mantra as a clever trick to outwit nature or the world of folly. The power of the mantra is not available to our employment but offers us employment in its power. At the instant of the mantra's springing up, there is a fractional second of choice, perhaps similar to Castaneda's cubic centimeter of chance. We can go with the mantra within or with the world without. Perhaps we prepare for this instant choice by our continual saying of the mantra to ourself. We get ready for those rare instances (rare in the beginning of our learning) when the mantra leaps up of itself to bail us out of some difficulty. The Gospels admonish us to "Be alert—for you never know at what instant *He* is coming." The instantaneous decision we must make is made entirely by our will; it tests the keen edge of our real ability. We can't rationally think over the issue, weigh the evidence, and opt for the most likely winner. Reason is light-years too slow for this split moment.

The mantra, which is my true Self, leaps up at that instant when I am about to lose myself to some situation; when I am about to fall into the world; when my ancient flight-fight syndrome is about to take over and lock my brain and senses into some outer stimuli supposedly threatening my well-being. If I say no to the mantra and yes to instinct I am lost in my physical senses and shut off from the power of consciousness within me, the only power for real change available. Then all I can do is pit my weak physical energy and weak emergent thought, made of its samskaras, against the far greater power of nature or my social world. Immediately, I am subject to the mechanics of that all-too-mechanical process, an arena of combat in which we all, sooner or later, always lose.

When our will has the ability to say yes to the mantra, though, we align with its power. Our brain is brought into resonance; it goes into balance between inner power and outer expression, and processes data without interpretation or value—which means it operates free of samskaras. Then outer stimuli feed directly into the power of consciousness and the creative circuitry of mind/brain can operate as a unit. Since consciousness is powering the outer world by projection through the brain anyway, the balanced brain simply allows for a balanced picture to form. When our brain is brought to balance by the mantra we are again at the center of the system, as designed. We have become ego-centric again. We have become again as a little child. The mantra is matrix.

We are then aligned with our Self, a person and world in balance. We are a unified whole which can't, because of its very nature, divide against itself. (The house divided against itself must surely fall.) The Self can't act against itself and, at the moment of balance (I believe) nothing inappropriate can occur. *But*—and this is the critical qualification—such results are peripheral, after-the-fact, incidental to and never parts of the computation of the moment of unity.

This moment of unity is true concrete operational thinking. This is the way the Ceylonese walk fire without harm, or run skewers through their cheeks without blood or pain. This is the way the Guru protects us if we can accept that protection. This is why Jesus of the fourth Gospel promised total invulnerability to his followers. And this is what, in our pitiful state of fracture, we have dimly glimpsed and referred to wishfully as "mind over matter," a hilarious misnomer made in ignorance.

Now John makes sense to me in those oft-quoted phrases: In the beginning was the Word, and the Word was with God, and the Word was God. Now I know why Jesus considered words the most important element of our life; why he said we are "judged by every word that comes out of our mouths." Now I know why the newborn infant responds to words with precise synchrony of movement, and why speech is genetic to our species. Now I sense what Muktananda means when he continually insists that the mantra *is* God. Mantra isn't a semantic label standing *for* God, Baba says, God and his name, like God and his creation, are the same.

So the primordial sound is still sounding, and the thing and its name are, at the primary level of creation, always of a piece. The Word lifts order out of chaos, and that lifting is always of this instant moment, the eternal now; and the big-bang cosmologists are right, if for the wrong reason, and rather in spite of themselves.

The ego-centric child's universe builds as a unison of word and thing, and that unison is the truth of our experience; the holonomic movement is always in unity. We separate name and thing, perhaps as we must separate our awareness of self from God, for the adventure of logical construction, discovery, relationship—and for the joy of reunion and merger, coming full circle again.

XIV

Eternity and Time

William Blake said: "Eternity is in love with the productions of Time." Or, in less poetic terms, the subtle orders of energy are in love with the gross physical; insight and consciousness are in love with thought; heart with head; God with Man; Shiva with Shakti.

The overall thrust of our personal development is for us to grow free of all physical processes, including world, body, and brain. What, though, could power our mind or furnish it its contents, on death of the brain?

The answer is, of course, that which has powered things all along. The holonomic order is always a unity; and there is always only the one source, the energy of consciousness guided by insight-intelligence.

Development is so designed that by old age, we should have established a firm working relationship with, or *bonded* with, our upcoming nonphysical matrix, just as an infant bonds with its mother. Bonds are made of consciousness and should be developed throughout life, right along with the capacity for independent thought.

Life in the physical world is designed to build a matrix of physical experience out of which a nonphysical experience can be drawn. The acquiring of experience is the acquiring of the ability to handle that kind of experience. The *content* of experience is incidental to the *ability* gained for handling it. The content of perception gives existence its shape, but content is transitory, disappearing as it forms. The perceptual ability which grows out of experience is what determines the nature of our ongoing experience. Our ability to perceive is the lasting part of our personality—the instrument of mind that life on this earth is designed to develop.

Information is of the weak, explicate order of energy, and is expendable. The ability to *process* that information is of the subtle, implicate order of energy, and is permanent within us. The shaping forces are the implicate forces, that which is shaped is explicate.

Ability may be the key to what happens to us in the next matrix, not some divine decree. If there is no capacity for nonphysical creativity, how could there be a successful matrix-shift to a nonphysical realm? For at death, when the physical body (and its world) collapses, instruments of the mind capable of relating to the nonphysical are needed.

Some people get upset by this observation, insisting that there are fixed, preset, and permanent "abodes" awaiting us after death. Perhaps there are, but even so, perception of that supposed realm, like any perception anywhere, would be a creative act, an ability of the instruments of the mind. The one thing that we can see from a study of infant/child development is the simultaneity of the development of intelligence and construction of the world.

Even should there be some fixed abode up-yonder, we must have the conceptual mechanism for perceiving it; which means, in effect, constructing it. Indeed, our perceptual development we make in the flesh almost surely determines that nature of the abode we finally perceive up-yonder (as it so seriously determines what we perceive down here).

No development can take place after death unless there is sufficient development in life. Perception results from concepts which are brain patterns formed from our sensory interactions with our world. Our subtle and causal bodies are the receptors of this perceptual action and can only perceive to the extent of our physical conceptual development.

The subtle body seems to be a mirror of the physical, an ability system that develops as we develop physically, and is subject to the limitations of that development. When I am in a subtle or causal state, I seem to perceive in an ordinary way (though what I perceive is seldom ordinary). Experiments by Charles Tart, Robert Monroe, and others clearly show that there are nonphysical stimuli which our subtle body can receive and perceive. Most people around Muktananda, or one of his centers, find this clearly the case, since an early stage of meditation seems to hinge around the subtle state (as later stages definitely go beyond it).

We learn to die by learning to live fully and perfectly. Each stage of life, each instant of existence, is a perfect expression of life as that (the child is not an incomplete adult). As Whitman said, ". . . the simple quahog in its shell were enough." The wonder is that something more is always forthcoming; for eternity can't fix itself in time.

Development requires that we fully experience each of the developmental matrices as we grow. To deny or restrict experience is to curtail development. Then there is an inadequate matrix-shift; capacity fails; death becomes a grim specter rather than the logical result of a growth process. Since all learning takes place from the concrete to the abstract, the creative process must be developed ahead of time to function after death of the body. Learning can take place abstractly only when capacities *for* abstraction have been built up sufficiently out of concrete experience. Unless the strength of mind (i.e., the proper instruments of mind) is developed to handle creativity in the comparative weakness of the physical world, the far stronger forms of the subtle or causal will surely be beyond us.

Nature provides us with the bonds to each next matrix, for matrix-shift is the way of growth and development. There is a dynamic interplay between implicate and explicate orders, between thought and consciousness. Since consciousness is the energy giving birth to thought, thought and consciousness should bond and interact just as mother and child should. But thought gets split off from consciousness, and isolated into its own self-generation, from which it can't extricate itself. This is the Fall. Once fallen, only the power of consciousness can reinstate the union, as only the power of the mother can move for the helpless infant.

Separation without relationship, loss of the power of the bond, breeds anxiety. The whiny, clinging, tearful, and obnoxious brat; the cruel, destructive, and undisciplined youngster; the defiant, surly, antisocial teenager; the alcoholic and depressed adult—all are trapped in the anxiety of alienation. A bonding not made at birth makes further bondings more and more unlikely. Somewhere after age seven, consciousness is largely lost and only verbal thought remains, its roof-brain chatter trying to fill a vacuum beyond its power. Personality remains grounded in the grossest and weakest of energies, related only to the body and physical matter; autonomy does not develop; matrix-shifts do not take place; with nowhere established to go after a physical life, death seems annihilation rather than being born out of the physical matrix into the freedom of creation.

A successful birth can't take place from the womb unless uterine development has prepared for that exodus. In the same way, a true birth out of the physical life can't take place at death unless development is sufficient. Perhaps one is not stillborn, but the ongoing life is surely crippled and inadequate. The subtle body is the repository of the whole error-ridden mess of physical life. Rather than developed as an instrument of mind and Self, the subtle body usually remains a confused replica of the physical. If we haven't caught on and learned to be an instrument of our whole being while in the body, we certainly can't in the subtle state, since learning is from the concrete to the abstract.

Indications from subtle experiences suggest that undeveloped personalities try to maintain their physical images in that subtle realm. The subtle realm becomes a vast, cosmic dumping-ground, a true garbage can for the continual and ongoing failure of the human venture to get beyond its sensory-motor development.

Bob Monroe has given an account of the immediate afterdeath subtle state. That strange eighteenth-century genius, Emanuel Swedenborg, apparently managed to cross back and forth into the subtle state. The inhabitants there seem to continue to be their own undeveloped selves.

The mother of my children died when our fifth child was less than a year old. This child was the "cerebral-palsy basket case" I mentioned earlier. The child's mother was completely locked in on her emotionally, unable to deal with the grim medical prognosis which the severe cerebral damage indicated (and certainly bore out). After my wife died, she made five manifestations back into our life, all in regard to this damaged child. In two cases, she appeared in striking visual form, staring intently, over the crib, at the child. In another episode, the child's grandmother had the infant's crib next to her own bed. The mother appeared in the night, bent over the crib. The close proximity nearly froze the grandmother, literally drew the heat from her body, paralyzing her. Had the manifestation lasted longer than it did, the grandmother felt she must surely have died herself. In two manifestations, the mother manipulated the infant's body; in one striking case causing the infant to sit bolt upright, stare intently at a designated area, and give, very graphically, a symbolic sign that had been an "in joke," or closed private communication between my wife and myself. This was the first, and the very last, body movement the child was ever to make. (She lived for several years.)

After some three months, the manifestations ceased. I don't believe anyone really knows the mechanics or principles of the ordinary subtle state. Bob Monroe's experiences indicate that state is vast and almost infinitely varied. And I know that, under sufficient emotional pressure, people there manage to break back into the ordinary, physical world in some kind of quasiphysical way.[1]

A fractured, undeveloped personality is little better than a bundle of samskaras, tendencies, half-baked abilities, personal memories, sentiments, and ego-posturings. Perhaps all that could happen at death is for such a personality to try again. Since learning and development can only take place from the concrete to the abstract, from the physical to the purely mental, when the physical breaks down, that bundle of confusion must be run through the system again. The potter must get some new clay and spin that wheel again. The carry-over into a rerun couldn't be the old clay, the content of memory and personality-image, but the *ability* (such as it were) gained in turning and firing the previous pot. Perhaps to the self it makes no difference—personalities can be grown by the billions. Mind has no content other than its instruments, or abilities, and the goal is development or perfection of those instruments.

Perfection isn't so much a matter of how many superabilities we have, as how free of distorting tendencies, compulsions, or attachments we are. When free of compulsion or attachment, any ability can be used to its fullest and can merge with mind in a smoothly functional whole. Then personality, as a complete development, becomes the general instrument of mind, and so an aspect of the Self's awareness of itself. Creator and creature become one not by a personality "seizing the tiller of the world," but by being so seized, becoming a true instrument. Only personality identified with Self endures.

Incomplete personalities may dissipate not on the death of the physical body, but on rebirth into another one, on that next go-round trying to shake samskaras and develop ability. Ability is a subtle energy, since a shaping force. Fractured ability is also a subtle energy. Once formed, subtle energies of this sort are "enfolded" within the subtle body and will always "unfold" in a physical life. Such automatic repetitiveness can be routed out only by a stronger energy, which is a principal role of the Guru operating through the Kundalini-Shakti.

During an intensive one weekend in June of 1979, I dropped (actually I felt I had been forcibly pushed) into a deep meditation from which I immediately emerged. I "woke up," more or less, but my brain didn't; my body didn't; the world didn't. It was given me to awake as a single point of clarity. This clarity was *me,* a *me* I had always been. (For some reason, I identify the state with my fifth and sixth years.) This me-awareness was complete and perfect beyond description. I was absolutely *me,* but had no name, no history, no body, space, time, or such. I was totally rich and perfect, nothing was lacking, although there *was* nothing. The state was not ecstatic as in a religious experience. It was nothing except perfection, without qualities; nothing could have been added or subtracted. It was everything conceivable and yet nothing at all.

I was allowed to remain in this lucid state of awareness for some time. Then I was led through a precise unfolding of creation from impulse of energy to vibration, to sound and light, space, time, and matter as proposed in Kashmir Shaivism, Baba's principal point of reference. Eventually, I found myself again in a body, though still as a point of clarity without a history. I was then expected, from some sort of inexorable logic within this lesson being given, to locate myself. I had no concept of location and couldn't make my brain give me one. This concept had to be "given me," rather as a switch being flipped on in my brain. This helped little since I had no vague notion of where I was. This information, too, finally had to be switched on for me.

The longest part of this rather long lesson then took place when I had to identify myself. Again that aspect of my brain was not available to me. I had no concept of self-identity. I was still a simple state of clarity, though in a body in a world in a specific place. A concept of identity had to be given as well, and again this helped nothing since I had no memory at all of being a somebody, or an "I."

This business of identity was not only withheld from brain-processing, but I began to sense that I really didn't want to know; for some reason, this seemed garbage I could do without. Such a conclusion did it; the switch flipped on and my personal history flooded me with a rush: my name, lineage, self-image, attachments, general nonsense and insanities. I then laughed, of course, at such a prolonged state of failure to remember something so basic as who I am.

Though I wanted nothing to do with it, when my identity flooded me, I *identified* with it instantly, without choice. Then I was no longer perfect, rich, and full. I then had all sorts of "things"—and had lost everything. I understood then that to identify with our social-ego image, our body, and the explicate order is truly folly. I knew then that we must instead identify with our Self and be willing to be its instrument. For in some way, mind, Self, and that point-of-clarity *me* are all of a piece. Yet my identity, my personality, is also an instrument of mind, *were it developed and matured.* And its only way of development to maturity is through being an instrument of mind and Self (against which we have been so thoroughly vaccinated).

Surely after my experience as this point of clarity, I knew that this identity I hold to, that I am so fearful of losing, can be thrown away like a pair of old name-tags, and it won't make the slightest whit of difference to *me.* This perfect point of clarity will never change. It is always here at the core and is always *me.* Surely I lose this casual attitude, but once having been stripped down to this core-me, once having experienced this true identity, I can never totally unknow it. I touch on it in meditation, and through the guidance of my Guru model-teacher, work goes on beneath the surface to turn my messy tendencies into abilities. For on being awakened by a true Guru, the Shakti within us starts systematically removing that deadly collection of tape-looped tendencies pulling us down to despair and defeat (just as the above meditation experience removed several serious blocks of my doubt, ignorance, and general anxiety). So, who knows: perhaps this fearful bundle of ego-identifying with name and history might get straightened out after all, and wedded to that rather nonchalant *me* lurking in there somewhere, and not have to be so expendable after all.

The world is the material out of which our creative ability should arise, while in our undeveloped state it is the matter against which we stumble. Creation fails when the materials for perception freeze into matter locked in time and space. Cleansing the doors of perception (of which Blake spoke) reinstates the world as the materials *for* perception. Rudrani Farbman's Shaktipat experience of the world melting into blue consciousness from which she could articulate form and matter at will is an example of the cleansing process beginning its work.

Muktananda sees the creation as a great burst of love and joy. *Maya* is a Sanskrit term for our perceptual illusion that sees reality as an unalterable concreteness happening to us as fate. But Maya is not our delusion about an unreal world. It is our failure to perceive that the world is material for an ongoing creation. Maya indicates a failure of nerve, where we don't accept responsibility for what we see, but try to see a fixed matter for which we need *not* be responsible.

Muktananda says you either see the world in its frozen state or you see God. So every day, without fail, he exhorts us, over and over again, to "see God in each other." He challenges us to move beyond the frozen world of matter, which is always hell, into the fluid world of creation. It takes a powerful imaginative strength to burst beyond the bind of paranoia which views the other person through the samskaras of hostility, fear, prejudice, envy, jealousy, and see that other person as God.

Walt Whitman wrote in "Song of Myself":

> *Why should I wish to see God better than this Day?*
> *I see something of God each hour of the twenty-four, and each moment*
> *   then,*
> *In the faces of men and women I see God, and in my own face in the*
> *   glass,*
> *I find letters from God dropt in the street, and every one is sign'd by*
> *   God's name,*
> *And I leave them where they are, for I know that wheresoe'er I go,*
> *Others will punctually come for ever and ever.*

Muktananda forcibly reminds us daily that this is not idle poetic fancy but the very gist of life and our own gateway to seeing God as our own Self within.

To create is to perceive in a fluid, dynamic state. When we die, the patterns of our physical world give way—for us they dissolve back into the subtle order from which they arose. Existence and perception being the same, for us to exist beyond life in the body, we must have a matrix beyond our physical world: a source of perceptual possibility; a safe space to explore that possibility; and a source of energy for that exploration. The subtle-causal realms offer this, just as they offered it for the construction of our physical world as infants. The problem doesn't lie with the matrix, but with our ability to shift into it.

Perception is creation and can use any source of materials for that creation: the world constructed from birth; the world of imaginative creation drawing *on* the world of experience; a consensus of imaginative creations shared with others; and the very implicate-causal order itself. All these are fluid states out of which reality may be lifted. We may "misplace concreteness" and miss the point of development if we assume that some ready-made given state after death is the point of life. The implicate-causal order is potential. To move into potential, we leave that which has already been realized.

We are created to develop the ability to create. The creature is designed to mature into the creator, the Son into the Father. The Creation is the way by which God the One becomes many, and why Eternity is in love with the productions of Time.

Muktananda, in his visions leading to his enlightenment, visited a state he calls Siddha Loka. This is a realm where he saw all the great Siddhas, the perfected masters of the past. They were represented to him sitting quietly, eyes closed, in meditation, under the "Wish-Fulfilling Tree." Under this tree, according to tradition, anything capable of being imagined is immediate reality. From Baba's accounts, we can detect some of the splendor inherent within such a capacity, but at the base of all the experiences recounted lies the foundation of reality-experience from the physical world. The creative process must have some germ of a notion around which its vast resources can be organized, and our creative process can only grasp that which our conceptual system can organize into perceptions—the two are synonymous effects.

Memory from physical life may give the basis for the development of this capacity for final autonomy. Once developed, once mind builds its own reservoir of potential material, even physical memory might become superfluous—no longer needed as a starting point. For instance, a friend related this story:

In his mid-thirties, his wife died. Several months later, an attractive young woman came to live with him. One evening, after having had intercourse with her, he lay awake pondering the strange "post-coitus blues" he always experienced. His young lover noticed his restlessness and began to make overtures for a repeat performance (such are the ways of youth), but he gently disengaged and turned his back to her, absorbed in the nature of this after-intercourse depression.

Immediately after he had turned from his young lover, with her pressed against his back, and with no shift of awareness as in drifting off into a dream-state, *another* person formed, in front of and directly against him. With a soul-wrenching recognition, he knew it to be *Her. She* was his *anima,* his female counterpart who had often appeared to him in dreams during time of stress, giving guidance, comfort, and a feeling of wholeness. *She* encompassed his earliest childhood sweetheart; his first great explosion of teenage love; his dead wife, mother of his children; his earliest impressions of his own mother; woman herself—mother and goddess; the genesis of all things; the rising of the first sun. Above all, *She* was the one he had always *known,* and the one who had always known him.

His joy at her forming there in his arms broke beyond his boundaries. Her lips, breasts, arms, and body struck him as waves of ecstatic flow melting into him in indescribable sweetness and joy of recognition, rediscovery, reunion after long parting. Coupled in a mystical ecstasy, they parted from Earth and fell through pulsating universes.

Finally she began to fade from him; she simply evaporated. This seemed impossible to bear and in his agony, he wept uncontrollably. For a while afterward, he could still sense the impress of her lips on his and then that, too, was gone.

He misinterpreted the experience, and it nearly ruined him. That such phenomena could exist, could take place, could be given, and yet were so rare (and he sensed this one would never come again), seemed hideous and a mockery. That sex could mean—had been—this, perhaps had always even been supposed to have been this, made sex as he had known it a farce and a travesty. And not just sex, but everything else in life paled to insignificance before the hugeness of that event. He was unable to maintain even a cordial relationship with his young paramour after that, and could explain his withdrawn and ensuing moroseness to no one. For some three years afterward, he maintained absolute celibacy and accelerated an ongoing spiritual journey.

Here all the given materials were from ordinary experience but were transformed into a whole far greater than the sum of those parts—which seems always to be the role of the creative process that mirrors back our will and passion. My friend had experienced a "sexual postulate" arriving full-blown in the brain, where sex had, as Blake insisted, become a divine and mystical union partaking of that divine union of Shiva and Shakti through which universes of experience are born. While it is hard to find a similarity of this with most sex, nevertheless, my friend's mystical phenomenon was drawn from the materials of a most mundane worldly act. And so it might be that all our mundane acts might furnish the seed from which far greater creations can then spring.

Muktananda exhorts us to turn within to experience a vast wealth. He claims that if we enjoy music, that we have no inkling of how great music can be until we hear the *inner* music always sounding there for us. That if we enjoy the smell of a rose, that such is insignificant compared to the wonderful aromas our inner world holds, and so on. And most of us glimpse, on occasion, at least fragments of what he speaks, enough to urge us on in our practice. But in every case, the germ of experience arises from the mundane world—which, it seems, is the purpose of this world, and why Eternity loves it.

There is, surely, an element of tragedy to the human race; not so much from the suffering and terror of so much of life as the uselessness of that suffering; not so much from the perceptual poverty and dullness of so much of our life as the unbelievable richness of experience that goes untapped. A negative whirlpool seems to pull us down into darkness, and surely it takes an enormous energy of imaginative creation to pull us out and free us from that negation. But, since Eternity *is* in love with Time, that energy is sent us, indeed is always present right within us, by which this freedom is attained. We must, however, first recognize the nature of our enslavement, and desire passionately, with all our heart, to be free.

XV

Vertical Alignment

Burton White, of Harvard's Child Development Center, found that about one child in every thirty was brilliant and happy. (A percentage that leaves nearly 97 percent of us dull and sad.) These bright children are from a wide variety of backgrounds and have only one detectable factor in common: all spend much of their time in *open, blank staring* (not precociously reading the *Encyclopedia Britannica* and filling every moment with busyness).

The Australian Aborigine stands on one leg, the other tucked against his thigh, his spear a balance-point against the Earth. Open-eyed, he goes into Dream-Time where he merges with the Two Great Brothers who instant by instant eternally found the Earth. He dissolves into the continuum of his holonomic order; lines of demarcation are erased. Flies crawl unmolested across his eyeballs, not because of stoic self-control (which he surely has), so much as because the fly is an extension of his body in its larger sense. In this state of unity, the Aborigine can unfold "enfolded" information as needed, and renew his life through euphoria and peace.

Blank, open-eyed staring is natural *meditation*. The child, like the Aborigine, doesn't need to close his eyes for meditation, since the world out there is an extension of his own being. The mind/brain is projecting the world out from its Self, and the child's and Aborigine's long periods of do-nothing staring maintain this unbroken unity, this egocentricity.

The child, like the Aborigine, is not thinking at this time. He is being. He is not thought but consciousness. To those in wholeness, the Creation is not only the "larger body of man," but one's own body. Here is individuation without isolation, I-ness without loss of the bonds of consciousness, the awareness of Self playing on the surface as a named identity.

Nature doesn't intend to plunge the young person from one matrix to another without proper bonding, since this would defeat development. Throughout the period from four to seven (and beyond), the mind/brain bonds (or tries to) with the Earth. These bonds are consciousness, not thinking, and never have to be articulated.

The brilliant child is that rare one who maintains his conscious unity with the holonomic order while functionally separating as independent thought. It isn't just coincidental that internal speech, or verbal thinking, doesn't begin to take over until after age seven, after that brain growth-spurt and shift of logic that gives a sense of individuality distinct from the world. The brilliant child, like the Uganda infant, separates without isolation and so is free of anxiety. Since the world is an extension of the unified Self, how can an extension of Self threaten?

Free of anxiety, the child's energy turns toward development rather than patching up his world or defending himself against it. The anxiety-free brain is a true tool at the service of development, not a defense weapon. An anxiety-free brain can learn at an astonishing rate, since learning is not a consciously aware, manipulated process, and anything to be learned is always within the brain's holonomic structure anyway. (Is all learning recognition, as long ago proposed?) When free of anxiety, development fills the sets of expectancy built over three billion years, and everything is right with that person. He is happy because his alignment with the orders of energy is maintained. He is where he is supposed to be, wherever he is—the world is his playground.

The brilliant happy child is not responsible *for* the world, but only for his response *to* the world. He can move toward dominion

over the world without the anxiety-driven attempt to try and dominate it. When our system unfolds as planned, the vast machinery of
body, brain, and world takes care of itself and allows the emergence
of a personality who can play on the surface and move beyond it
when the time comes.

When the system malfunctions, the person on the surface is
afraid to play and create. He turns back in anxious work to try and
repair the machinery. He tries, in fact, to take over the explicate machinery and run it. His idea of discipline is to control more of his
exterior world, which includes his neighbor. Because this is such a
misapplication of thinking, disaster falls about his head. He is
caught in the error-correction error, which produces only minuses
and madness.

When blank staring takes place before a TV screen (as it does for
our 97 percent dull and sad), the child bonds to the chaos of that
screen. He is not being egocentric as designed by nature, but exo-
centric—he is being constantly pulled outside his center. The *screen*
is the center of his world and impinges upon him. Whether this im-
pingement is cartoon mayhem, commands to buy corn flakes, in-
structions on how to spell Sesame Street or read the encyclopedia, *is
absolutely of no consequence.* The content is inconsequential—the
formal device itself and its effect is all that counts—and all that will
ever count. No content can be conceived that can overcome the dramatic split of Self that the mechanism itself induces.

The anxiety-ridden child may have never been allowed his egocentricity; never allowed to be the quiet witness of his world. Unless
he is allowed dominion over his projected world, by being allowed
to be totally a child in a complete and perfect ego-centeredness—
rather than an object of instruction or "reality-adjustment"—this,
his universal construction itself, will not be complete. Then his construction of a personality to play on the surface will not be complete. Mind will not get its instruments. That person will lose the
best of both worlds, child and adult, and will lock into a fragmented
isolated ego.

A sense of I-ness, or ego, was never meant to be an error, a grim
sentence of death, an unleashing of a terror on the social world and
destruction on the good Earth. I-ness was meant to be the "grape

bursting in the throat" from an exuberance unable to contain its joy, power, ecstasy, and delight over having projected a universe in which to play and create. I-ness was meant to become a Baba Muktananda who understands that consciousness is play. (We all knew this as children, had flashes of it in lightning moments of our teens, lost our vision of it in our twenties, and plunged to despair.)

Anxiety freezes the mind/brain into a negative kind of one-pointedness: the single compulsion to get out from under that anxiety. This compulsion swamps all circuitry, stops all intelligence in its tracks, and sets up a tape-looped warp that influences the way our perceptual reality forms. Our thoughts are emergents of this locked-up system and can't produce except in accord with it. (We set up a criterion based *on* this deadly fixation and call it our Intelligence Quotient and boast of our child's IQ.) We hail the great scientific "breakthroughs," discoveries, and achievements produced in our anxiety-search and wonder why each milestone of progress crumbles into tomorrow's nightmare.

The brilliant child is aligned with his three orders of energy: thought, consciousness, and insight-intelligence. His meditative spaces keep this order aligned. Eventually, the inroads of acculturation warp this alignment and cloud the scene; but even so, his early capacities, while diverted to cultural madness and defeating the plan of life, are never completely extinguished; so even his warped cultural actions are "brilliant" within the low-average norm of his culture.

Meditation for adults, as taught by Muktananda, is partially remedial of necessity. The goal is alignment of the orders of the holonomic system. To do this, thought must be trained as an instrument of mind, which means the brain must be reorganized, freed of the action of samskaras. This the awakened Shakti immediately sets about to do. (It's not an overnight process.)

Meditation trains thought to be one-pointed in the face of the brain's continual barrage of sensory impressions and desires. To do this, the brain must be freed from its one-pointed lockup in anxiety. The only way we can be freed of anxiety is to be shown or given an actual inner demonstration of an inner source of peace and power greater than that we might think we can get through manipulations of our outer world. This is the "grace" of Shaktipat or perhaps eventual meditation experience which so dramatically transforms the attitudes of Siddha students.

Meditation trains us in discrimination: sensing what is right and wrong. This was a problem for me, for in the world of folly these terms are truly "relative" and meaningless. But that which leads toward or maintains alignment between the orders of energy is Truth. That which leads away from this alignment is False, no matter that it might be consistent within itself. Science, for instance, often delineates a "truth" about the physical world which is actually only a tautology—true only within the tight confines of the circular definition science sets up to produce this "truth." In its treatment of the physical as the only reality available, its isolating of thought into self-generating circles, *all* the works of science prove functionally false and breed destruction and terror—sooner or later. (Just as any work or discovery of science could be *actually* true and so beneficial were it created in the service of, and so in alignment with, the holonomic movement.)

Alignment can only come through our turning within to the center of order. Oriented to the center, all falls into place and we can then move through the continually unfolding outer world without loss of our identity to that world. Then our criterion or discrimination comes from the realm of insight-intelligence, not the outer manifestation, and we maintain our alignment.

Meditation develops *will*: the ability and desire to hold to one-pointedness and discrimintion in the face of confusions and distractions. *Will* is the sum of our personal power and a subtle energy which can alter the explicate order. Once the world has fallen and the mass of men are oriented to their outer folly and its chaos, to move through this without distraction is a work of art.

Will also means *willingess*. We must allow the holonomic order to function through us without our surface thought becoming self-generative and trying to take over, which takeover would immediately shift us from wholeness into the fragmentation of the surface struggles. Should this happen, we would then only contribute to the fragmentation, no matter how noble our intent. Strength of mind is the ability to hold one-pointedly, discriminate with alertness, and step graciously aside and serve what is given as appropriate in the moment's unfolding.

Meditation aligns the three levels of our being in a way that can carry us far beyond the possibilities of our weak brain processes when left to themselves. Left on its own, our shifting social-ego bows to myriad pressures from without. Focused without, guilty and anxiety-ridden, the gears don't mesh, nothing works right. Focused within, all gears mesh and everything works. That's why meditating people seem both happier and more efficient. They don't depend on their surface thought alone; though below their level of awareness, they are aligned—to some extent, at least—with power and insight, which is to say, they are aligned with the Guru.

Siddha Yoga meditation is an exercise in perfection. The emphasis is not on the occasional great act, but on the greatness of every act. Whether peeling an onion, keeping one's room or bank account straight, or writing the Great American Novel, all acts are equal and all must be equally perfect—performed to the fullest of capacity.

Baba sends us back into our worldly roles for just this reason. He tells us that there is no other ground for our learning *than* this world. Nearly all of us go through a period when, discovering the joy and peace of chanting, the profound experiences of meditation, we resent the intrusion of the mundane world. To handle the powerful energies of the subtle and causal realms, however, we must build sufficient mental muscles in the physical. Baba never lets us forget this balance. Ashram life itself balances between meditation and chanting, and plain ordinary work—all of which we finally learn to treat as identical. That is, there finally comes (I am *told*—that is) a time when chopping onions for hours on end *is* meditation and a source of peace and joy.

Back in 1976, following my own Shaktipat experience from Baba's picture, I "renounced the world" and all its works, determined never again to fool with lecturing or book-writing. Yet in 1979, following a summer of study in Siddha Yoga, events were such that I just started accepting invitations (perhaps grudgingly) again. Then I was told that Baba had "suggested" I might like to write a book about my Siddha Yoga venture. This really disturbed me since I was so new to Siddha Yoga, knew little, and dreaded the "head trip" and preoccupation book-writing demands. I longed to bask in "spiritual matters." Shortly after his suggestion, though, the book fell into my head one morning in meditation. I saw it as a whole, complete and perfect. Thinking of Mozart and his conception of a new work, I enthusiastically pulled out my typewriter. And I drew a blank. I couldn't recall what I had seen with clarity so shortly before. Blake said, "Mechanical excellence is the vehicle of genius," and, alas, such excellence was not mine. So I went back to studies and notes. The next morning, the same thing happened, and this went on for weeks.

I began to sit arbitrarily for a couple of hours daily, typing away at a book-of-sorts. The results were awful—not one line ever proved worth keeping. This went on for four months, and suddenly one day, following a couple of weeks away for travel and lectures, everything meshed. This book commenced and went well, with a firm (even compulsive) hold on me night and day.

My meditation may have functioned on two levels. Perhaps it held the goal before me, gave me glimpses, though I couldn't articulate them; and slowly (at least I wishfully believe) straightened out at least enough of the chaos in my head that thought could be used as an instrument—and kept out of the way when not.

In 1976, after "throwing everything out," I was convinced that I should strip my brain and start afresh (which is nonsense—thought can't erase itself). For three years, I avoided reading anything related to my old patterns of thinking. When I came to Baba, I was aware of the folly of bringing old trips with me. Faced with the genius and greatness I found Baba to be, I knew an honest embarrassment over my presumptuous books and notions of the past.

I found, though, to my surprise, that my months of failure to get *this* book going was tied in with my notion that I had to start from a blank state. Instead, this Baba-suggested book has proved a summary of my life and thought to this point. The fact is, the Guru wastes nothing. Opening to the whole order of our being, everything is transformed. All my old ideas are back, refurbished, straightened out a bit, and fitting into a more or less functional whole.

Blake proclaimed: "I must create a system of my own or be enslaved by another man's." I had never consciously set about to create a system—but from my earliest years (certainly from my second grade in school on), I was convinced of a certain set of facts: that what was happening to me (in school particularly) was unnatural and against my well-being; that God didn't mock his children, that the natural order of things was essentially good and perfect, and that a way for achieving this natural balance had to be available; that our essential nature was one of magnificence beyond imagining; the grim suffering and paucity of our lives, a monstrous misunderstanding.

And so, inadvertently, I "created a system of my own," only to find it always falling short. Finally, in my inner bankruptcy, I submitted to *being* enslaved by another man's system, and found, of course, to my surprise, that my willingness to *be* so enslaved was the vitally missing ingredient of my own system itself. Muktananda throws nothing away! He doesn't brainwash and pour some hypnotic potion into us. He is not here to enslave us to some system but to help us articulate our own. "You want to be a dancer?" he asks the young lady. "Fine, go dance. But be a perfect dancer, make dance your meditation. Be one-pointed and discriminating." Thus we find, in our once-mundane worldly activity, that our criterion has shifted. The audience is no longer the hostile critic of a paranoid world, but our inner Self, God himself, who is equally in every facet of that outer world as well.

Siddha meditation is the philosopher's stone that transmutes the rough dross of our life to gold; a catalyst to lift us out of chaos into order; a prism to bring our scattered light into clear focus.

I think of Western thought, its technology spreading over the world like a cancer, its skyrocketing epidemic of broken, damaged children and alcoholic adults, and I think of this infusion of Eastern thought presenting itself to us for acceptance. Surely there is a strong parallel here between left and right hemispheric thinking in the brain. Surely the East still represents, even now in its state of upheaval and cultural conflict, "left-handed thinking"—the thinking of wholeness and order, as opposed to the analytical, digital, and fragmenting thought of the West. And of all Eastern thinkers to venture into the West, Muktananda seems the first to be absolutely unswayed, unchanged *by* the West and yet the least interested in throwing Western thought out. Again, Baba wastes nothing—he transforms. Just as in my writing this book, finding my thought given back in a larger frame, the West could find its potentially great thought brought into true greatness through what Muktananda offers: an aligning with the holonomic order of things.

"You would be a scientist? Fine. Be a perfect one. Make science your meditation." But in so doing, to be perfect, to make of science a meditation, science would have to open to consciousness, insight, and intelligence; become an instrument of the creative process rather than trying to make creation *its* instrument.

Bringing meditation to the West may not be a Band-Aid to relieve a spiritual scratch, but the thinking Earth's move for self-preservation—and even a leap into a new domain. Western alienation may have developed a viewpoint, a way of thinking, that, *were it aligned with truth,* could lead to extraordinary heights.

Eternity is in love with the productions of Time, and Baba honors those productions. He says every act, word, thought is his worship of God. And this is the reason he sends us back into the world—because God is in love with this world, Eternity is in love with Time, Insight is in love with Thought.

Time, with its passionate thoughts here in our head, impregnates Eternity, that Shakti within our heart, that mother of all creation. And this is that mother's secret: whatever her lover gives her, she gives it back enlarged, strengthened, clarified, and greater than that given, since that is her creative, bountiful nature.

So Baba doesn't disparage action in this world; he teaches us that every act is art. He urges us, by example, to work for mechanical excellence and become the vehicle for our inner genius—that is, offer ourselves to our heart, enter that union by which the holonomic movement remains whole. For here is the consummate art, the goal of all goals and Muktananda's constant challenge: that we gather up, with passion and desire, the scattered fragments of our own life; and, through meditation, one-pointedly channel these fragments into that creative realm, that Primordial Principle in the cave of the heart; and be willing to serve with devotion the offspring of that union when it comes: the postulate of all postulates, a life greater than the sum we have to give.

Notes

INTRODUCTION

1. Nothing seems so futile as the "search for the historical Jesus," an aberration cropping up from time to time. The issue with Jesus is: Does he *address* us; does he move us to self-examination and the desire to change the fundamental structure of our life?

The issue Castaneda presents us is *not* "is or was Don Juan real?" The issue is, on reading Carlos do we acknowledge our need for radical change? The minute we shift to some logical argument about *Carlos,* his writing, or authenticity, we have evaded the real issue and, in effect, said NO to the spirit of life which Carlos has vitally represented.

Carlos's technique for writing *Tales of Power* (N.Y., Simon & Schuster, 1974) is revealing. He told a friend of mine that he organized his huge collection of notes into logical categories, rather than chronological sequence. He would select a particular category of phenomenon, immerse himself completely in it for days or weeks, until, at some point of saturation-exhaustion, he would fall asleep, more or less, and "dream the next chapter."

"Aha!" the psychologist exclaims. "So Carlos's work is fiction, and he is a fraud." Not so. Carlos's technique follows the pattern of all great creative thinking. As Blake made clear, the profundity of one's message cannot rise above the level of the vehicle within which that message is presented. What emerges need not be a one-for-one correspondence with the actuality of events in order to *represent* the truth. And all printed words are but representations. They can *only* imply. We, the reader, must do the creative work of making explicit that which is implicit within our own mind/brain, and the success of our efforts is largely dependent upon the success of the artist's original representation of his conception.

There are many times when, to represent the truth accurately, which means in a translatable way, we must select and synthesize from a wide body of pertinent information. A world of hard, cold facts, lying separate and distinct from what we make of it, is our greatest fiction. If we want people to read our representation, rather than being bored to death at the outset, we must cast it in a fashion worthy of interest. God knows, the world is a fantastic and incomprehensible experience anyway. Why represent our response to it in a stupid, mechanical way?

How *should* Carlos have represented his experience-idea-creative-intuitive-revelatory thought? In some dry, utterly dull and dead dissertation for a dry, utterly dead *psychological journal*? Further, there is always the possibility that, in spite of "evidence" presented by the picayune, Carlos was telling the truth. Lord knows, my own personal experience has touched on, in one way or another, almost every category of phenomenon Carlos wrote about. Touched lightly and briefly, granted, but enough to know "it" is there—or here.

Carlos was enough of a visionary artist to do as Plato did, and "suggest an infinity of responses" without compelling any. Millions read Carlos and were moved to change their lives within whatever framework afforded them *for* change. Many of those longing for change, looking for their Don Juan, have been led to Muktananda (as was I), and Carlos provided the door opening from a closed cultural impasse into a greater life. Very few people have a specific beneficial influence on their times. I think Carlos was one of those few. I can only reiterate Blake's apt observation: "He who calumniates great men calumniates God." Surely petty thinkers throw stones at great men—such is the fate of greatness. I doubt, though, that Carlos lives in such a glass house that he need be greatly disturbed.

CHAPTER I

1. The thrust of this book is to explain Shaktipat, so a definition of it must simply arise out of the context here.

CHAPTER II

1. All of my references to Northrop Frye are from his monumental work: *Fearful Symmetry: A Study of William Blake,* Princeton, N.J., Princeton University Press, 1947.

2. Pictures of Muktananda in his late thirties and early forties show a trim, muscular, almost athletic man. (He had been a Hatha Yoga expert for

years.) Pictures of him after his transformation show the same lean body, but with pendulous breasts and a distinctly advanced-pregnancy belly. Medical friends of mine have speculated on this strange phenomenon, how the estrogen-testosterone hormone balances have been upset, and so on. Muktananda is *the most masculine* personality I know, yet his body *does* look like that of a pregnant woman and he certainly *walks* like one.

Yogic explanation of this is that the "realized being" retains his *prana* or life-force within him. This might, I suppose, somehow account for that belly (Muktananda says it's only air), but hardly those breasts. The true Yogi is celibate and retains his semen within his body. Even our supposedly involuntary nocturnal seminal discharges can be stopped through an exercise of will, and certainly the Yogi exercises such a will. (I know this can be done, for I did it for a three-year period.) As one research person expressed it: the Yogi seems to impregnate his own person.

Consider that the brain is "essentially feminine" to begin with. The male creature is a bit of an anomaly at best. Perhaps the Yogi, on achieving "realization," returns to this basic, creative position, carrying with him the advantages gained by a male viewpoint. He then incorporates the best of both worlds. What is involved may be our ordinary sense of polarity on which we base all our reality. A conception of "things and events" seems to make necessary a play of opposites. That is, we can't seem to grasp the concept "heat" without "cold," "love" without "hate," and so on. Possibility seems to arise from this play. *But* in order to move *beyond* this learning process into the full creativity possible *from* this basis, the creative mind must free itself of the pull of polarity.

The incredible experiences endured by Muktananda in his nine years of transformation apparently obliterated the play of polarities in his conceptual system. Then he recognizes no differences, and all is consciousness, all is God, in his sight. That is, he isn't just speaking metaphorically when he insists all is consciousness without division; he is expressing his direct perceptual awareness. This means his brain structure has been correspondingly changed. And we know that a change of fundamental brain structure *must* be reflected in the body, since the body is an instrument of that brain. So, erase conceptual polarities, including that of male-female, and the body becomes *neither* male nor female. Thus it is safe to say that these "realized beings" are plugged into a different circuitry. Further, I submit that this peculiar, indeed bizarre, bodily change is one guideline to a genuine, authentic Guru person.

A final point here is that we probably must, at some point, move beyond sexuality in order to achieve this final maturity. Sexuality may well be a stepping-stone along the way, and the very "dawn of creation," but at some point that dawn must go down to day. Certainly we note that in ordinary physical maturation sexuality fades as a driving force. It should, of course, be replaced by nonphysical creation. Jesus claimed that "in the Kingdom of Heaven there is no marrying." A spiritual friend of mine claimed that this meant that the truly spiritual and realized person was entitled to open intercourse, or "free love" without the bonds of matrimony. Whether sexual love should be "free" or "bound" in matrimony is not the point. The point is that maturation of personality moves beyond the dualities and polarities of sexuality. (And there *are* areas of experience and phenomena vastly more compelling and intoxicating than sexuality.)

Naturally, in this day when anything beyond the physical world is both denied and perceptually undeveloped, sexuality is heralded as the final and last card to play. And we find the hilarious spectacle of ancient old couples trudging dutifully to the sex counselors to see if they can't get it on one more time. It used to be that we were made to feel guilty if we *had* sex. Now we are made to feel guilty if we don't even at ninety-five.

CHAPTER III

1. All references to David Bohm's holonomic order, Karl Pribram, and so on, can be found in *Re-Vision*, a journal of knowledge and consciousness, Vol. 1 #3/4, Summer-Fall, 1978.

CHAPTER IV

1. For an article on "auditory beats" see Gerald Oster, in the October 3, 1973, *Scientific American*. Let me add here that the Monroe Institute of Applied Science incorporates a wide variety of responses and their research goes far beyond exploration of the subtle-body states mentioned in this book. For instance, Monroe recently completed a highly successful "stroke recovery program" using the same hemispheric synchronization process by which, through a different usage, one can experience the out-of-body state. Monroe's work covers many areas. For information, write: Monroe Institute of Applied Science, P. O. Box 175, Faber, Va. 22938.

CHAPTER V

1. The words *culture* and *society* are defined differently according to professions. Sociologists seem to refer to societies as specific examples of a culture. Anthropologists or archaeologists tend to refer to cultures as generic. I decided to use the word culture, since *enculturation* implies a more powerful mind-set than socialization. I doubt my usage will please either group.

2. My first book, *The Crack in the Cosmic Egg*, was once called "the definitive work on fire-walking" (*The New York Times*). How sad. My book wasn't at all *about* fire-walking, nor was my explanation at all *the* definitive one. Indeed, I am only now beginning to grasp the complexities—and sim-

plicity—of this phenomenon. Still, all we need is one example of fire-walking to call the lie to the whole fabric of modern academic-scientific thought. You simply can't have fire-walkers and Carl Sagan both. They are mutually exclusive. On the one hand we have the bravado and bluster of the "mouth warrior," the champion of the semantic world of fiction-writing and semireal thinking; on the other hand a demonstration of a profound truth, the actual relation of mind and matter.

CHAPTER VI

1. I must refer the reader to my book *Magical Child,* for all references and sources used in this chapter. This single chapter incorporates most of the argument of *Magical Child,* and to document such a condensed form was simply not feasible.

CHAPTER VIII

1. The Fall happens to each of us anew in childhood. We aren't aware of it until after the fact, and then take our fall to be our natural state. Consider one simple example: most child-learning involves trial and error and many mishaps. All it takes is a few parental scoldings, condemnations, derogatory remarks concerning the child's efforts, to implant guilt, shame, a sense of inadequacy in that child. The parent is the child's criterion, his pattern for world-making and interpretation of his own emerging personality. If that source criticizes or makes fun of the natural process of world-view construction taking place, child-anxiety is the only possible result, since this sets up a conflict of signals, and a source of confusion and uncertainty. Jean Liedloff's description of a proper parental response is revealing. (See her *The Continuum Concept,* N.Y., Knopf, 1977.)

CHAPTER X

1. See John Ross, "The Resources of Binocular Perception," *Scientific American,* March 1976.

CHAPTER XI

1. Western confusion over the Holy Spirit, or Guru, and the relation of God and Man is well expressed in our confusion over the words *Jesus* and *Christ.* "The Christ" is a generic term; it refers to the function of the Holy Spirit or Guru, the guide who is always appearing in the flesh. Jesus was one of the specifics of this phenomenon. The function must have its explicate form. So, again, Jesus wasn't the Christ, the Christ was Jesus—as He was the Buddha, etc., and is always someone here and now. By the very

structure of reality the function of the Guru is always here, and always "coming again." Perhaps Augustine referred to this when he wrote: "That which is now called the Christian religion existed among the ancients, and never did not exist from the planting of the human race, until Christ came in the flesh at which time the true religion which already existed began to be called Christianity." That "that which is now called Christianity" is either that which "always existed" or that to which Jesus himself tried to point is extremely debatable, but Augustine points up the fact that a Guru-function, or Christ-function, is an inseparable part of human history.

CHAPTER XII

1. *Darshan* means "meeting with a saint." Each evening during the two-hour program the ashram holds, each meditation student lines up to personally meet Muktananda. The meetings are extremely brief, usually (hundreds are waiting), but questions can be asked, and much takes place. Muktananda very definitely "sees" each of us in a Carlos "Don Juan" way, intuitively grasping the general nature of our spiritual state, and picking up specific information as needed.

CHAPTER XIII

1. My information on Alfred Tomatis came from a transcript sent me of an Australian radio interview with Tomatis. Since then I have been sent a number of scientific papers of and about his work, as well as the work of his colleague, Dr. Guy Berard, who has been doing exceptional work with autistic children. The Metascience Institute, Box 191, Encinitas, Ca. 92024, is incorporating these French studies in their own research into human potential.

2. Carpenter and the singing gibbons of Thailand can be found in Sally Carrighar's *Wild Heritage,* Boston, Houghton Mifflin, 1965.

CHAPTER XIV

1. For most of us Westerners, locked into the perceptions of a physical body and world, with no way out but death, release into the subtle-body state can be the most profound experience of our lives. Bob Monroe's "training sessions" are important from that standpoint alone. No personality can be quite the same, or locked into the prevailing anxiety, after having a subtle-body experience. Nevertheless, the subtle body is but the first stage beyond the physical, is not the goal of development, and can be a serious sidetrack *to* development.

Interestingly enough, when a person becomes disenchanted with the world of folly, the madness of our social scene and its "rat race," that person usually follows a predictable cycle. This cycle follows, in rather shadow-form, the actual developmental stages unfolding in childhood. After disenchantment with the world of Nixons, Waynes, and atom bombs, enchantment with "psychic matters" usually follows. This indicates the attempt of the system to recoup that developmental period from about age four to seven, as expressed in telepathy, clairvoyance, general ESP, and so on. Then comes a period of more intense esoterica, moving objects by thinking, science-fictional "powers," mind over matter, and so on, all referring vaguely to *concrete operational thinking* that should unfold between about seven and eleven. Then comes rejection of these lesser things and a plunge into serious intellectual pursuit. Ouija boards give way to joining institutes and societies intellectualizing on human potential, all of which reflects on *formal operational thinking,* as designed to unfold between eleven and about fifteen. Finally, if the person is lucky and lives long enough, he works his way through even this and enters onto the actual path, the life of the spirit—moving toward true Reversibility Thinking, and actual maturity. One on this final path has no truck with the lesser stages, even as he might, occasionally, have to employ those earlier developments, or finds them employed on his behalf.

Bibliography

Muktananda:
Play of Consciousness, San Francisco, Harper & Row, 1978
Siddha Meditation, South Fallsburg, N.Y., SYDA Foundation, 1979
Reflections of the Self, South Fallsburg, N.Y., SYDA Foundation, 1980
I Am That, South Fallsburg, N.Y., SYDA Foundation, 1979
Meditate, Albany, N.Y., SUNY Press, 1980
In the Company of a Siddha, Oakland, SYDA Foundation, 1978
Kundalini: The Secret of Life, South Fallsburg, N.Y., SYDA Foundation, 1979

Bohm:
Truth and Actuality, N.Y., Harper's, 1978
Fragmentation and Wholeness (monograph), Van Leer Foundation, 1976

For information concerning the world-wide network of Siddha Meditation Centers, and ashrams, or to order Siddha publications, write:
SYDA Foundation
P.O. Box 605
South Fallsburg, N.Y. 12779
(212) 247-5573 or (914) 434-4850

Books of Related Interest

The Biology of Transcendence
A Blueprint of the Human Spirit
by Joseph Chilton Pearce

The Crack in the Cosmic Egg
New Constructs of Mind and Reality
by Joseph Chilton Pearce
Foreword by Thom Hartmann

From Magical Child to Magical Teen
A Guide to Adolescent Development
by Joseph Chilton Pearce

The Secret Dowry of Eve
Woman's Role in the Development of Consciousness
by Glynda-Lee Hoffmann
Foreword by Joseph Chilton Pearce

Profound Healing
The Power of Acceptance on the Path to Wellness
by Cheryl Canfield
Foreword by Joseph Chilton Pearce

The Yoga of Spiritual Devotion
A Modern Translation of the Narada Bhakti Sutras
by Prem Prakash

Inner Traditions • Bear & Company
P.O. Box 388
Rochester, VT 05767
1-800-246-8648
www.InnerTraditions.com

Or contact your local bookseller